CHEF MICHAEL SMITH'S KITCHEN

100 OF MY FAVORITE EASY RECIPES

CHEF MICHAEL SMITH

Photography by James Ingram

PINTAIL

PINTAIL
a member of Penguin Group (USA)

Published by the Penguin Group
Penguin Group (Canada), 90 Eglinton Avenue East, Suite 700,
Toronto, Ontario, Canada M4P 2Y3 (a division of Pearson Canada Inc.)

Penguin Group (USA) Inc., 375 Hudson Street, New York, New York 10014, U.S.A.
Penguin Books Ltd, 80 Strand, London WC2R 0RL, England
Penguin Ireland, 25 St Stephen's Green, Dublin 2, Ireland (a division of Penguin Books Ltd)
Penguin Group (Australia), 250 Camberwell Road, Camberwell, Victoria 3124, Australia
(a division of Pearson Australia Group Pty Ltd)
Penguin Books India Pvt Ltd, 11 Community Centre, Panchsheel Park, New Delhi – 110 017, India
Penguin Group (NZ), 67 Apollo Drive, Rosedale, Auckland 0632, New Zealand
(a division of Pearson New Zealand Ltd)
Penguin Books (South Africa) (Pty) Ltd, 24 Sturdee Avenue, Rosebank, Johannesburg 2196,
South Africa

Penguin Books Ltd, Registered Offices: 80 Strand, London WC2R 0RL, England

Published in Penguin paperback by Penguin Canada, a division of Pearson Canada Inc., 2011

Published in this edition, 2012

1 2 3 4 5 6 7 8 9 10 (CR)

Copyright © Michael Smith, 2011

Food Photography: James Ingram, Jive Photographic
Additional Photography: Loretta Campbell, vi, viii, 24, 48, 62–63, 72, 98, 112–113,
122, 136–137, 168, 200–201, 232, 256–257; istockphotos by Henk Badenhorst, 34–35;
Jim DeLillo, 88-89; and Sandy Jones, 252

Manufactured in the U.S.A.

ISBN 978-0-670-06691-9

Visit the Penguin US website at **www.penguin.com**

ALWAYS LEARNING

PEARSON

This book is for everyone

who gathers, prepares,

and shares food.

And to whoever cleans up the mess!

ALSO BY MICHAEL SMITH

Open Kitchen

The Inn Chef

Chef at Home

The Best of Chef at Home

CONTENTS

INTRODUCTION

Food is for sharing. Its ingredients, its creation, its flavours, and its stories are all at their best when experienced with our family, friends, and community. For many cooks, though, their food begins with words shared, with written recipes like the ones in this book.

Food is for creating. My goal is not for you to precisely duplicate how I might cook a dish but to share my ideas and insight so you can confidently create your own version of a dish. Your food doesn't have to look or taste like mine to succeed. When you cook a dish it becomes yours, whatever its inspiration or outcome, because as home cooks, success lies simply in going for it.

Food is fun. Over the years I've always enjoyed cooking. Letting yourself go—simply allowing your ingredients to guide you—is empowering and enjoyable. You can relax, smile, laugh, and stay in the moment. That's how your cooking becomes peaceful and gratifying and leaves you open to discovery.

Food is for exploring. I rarely cook the same dish the same way twice, but I often stumble onto variations that I find memorable. There are many ways to interpret an idea, but inevitably we all discover favourites. Those are the flavours I have chosen to share with you in this book.

Food is personal. It helps us be our best. It's anchored in time and place and always tells a story. Each of the following dishes was inspired by many stories, but the best is yet to come. Join the fun by cooking them and making them yours. That's the inspiration for all of the flavours in this book. They're for you. For your table. For your stories.

BREAKFAST

Brown Butter Scrambled Eggs, 3

Bacon Breakfast Taco with Cheddar Scrambled Eggs, 4

Potato Bacon Cheddar Breakfast Bake, 7

Smoked Salmon Quiche with Gruyère and Dill, 8

Apple Pie Pancakes with Caramel Syrup, 11

Caramel Apple "Flipjack", 12

French Toast Sandwiches Oatmeal Crusted with
Blueberry Stuffing and Marmalade Mint Butter, 15

Buttermilk Waffles with Cinnamon Apple Stew, 16

Extra-Blueberry Muffins with Brown Butter, 19

Vanilla Yogurt Muesli with Ten Fruits, Nuts, and Seeds, 22

BROWN BUTTER SCRAMBLED EGGS

Brown butter is my favourite flavour. Since it begins my day on a regular basis, it has the honour of beginning this chapter and this book of my favourite flavours. It's an essential flavour in every cook's repertoire and a metaphor for all great cooking. Patiently browning butter is a magical journey of flavour creation. You'll easily master the technique, then find yourself looking for any excuse to use brown butter in your cooking. Maybe that's why it appears at least five more times in this book. Here, it flavours simple scrambled eggs. **Makes 1 large serving that's easily doubled**

3 eggs, lightly beaten
2 tablespoons (30 mL) of water
A thinly sliced green onion, a sprinkle of sliced chives, or some chopped parsley
A pinch or two of salt and lots of freshly ground pepper
1 tablespoon (15 mL) of butter

Preheat your favourite heavy frying pan over medium heat. Meanwhile, toss the eggs, water, and green onion into a bowl and thoroughly whisk them together. Season the mixture with salt and pepper to your taste.

Drop the butter into the preheated pan. Gently swirl the works, helping the butter melt evenly. Watch as the water released from the melted butter foams and simmers away and the remaining butterfat rises in temperature and begins to lightly brown. Continue swirling. When the butter is richly fragrant and golden brown, pour in the eggs.

Scramble the eggs, stirring constantly with a wooden spoon or rubber spatula until they're creamy and thick, 2 to 3 minutes. Serve immediately.

KITCHEN TIP

Scrambled eggs are at their best when they're thick and creamy. Thoroughly whisking the eggs helps them maximize their natural tendency to become fluffy. A small amount of liquid generates inflating steam while adding tenderness. Constant stirring interferes with the inevitable tendency of the eggs to stick together, allowing a tender, creamy texture to emerge.

BACON BREAKFAST TACO WITH CHEDDAR SCRAMBLED EGGS

These tacos are a fun way to jazz up your breakfast table with some familiar flavours that usually show up later in the day. They're made the same way normal tacos are with one obvious exception: scrambled eggs easily replace meat. **Makes 8 tacos**

8 large taco shells
4 slices of bacon, cut into small chunks
6 eggs
1 heaping cup (275 mL) of grated Cheddar cheese
A pinch or two of salt and lots of freshly ground pepper
1/2 cup (125 mL) or so of your favourite salsa
A thinly sliced green onion
A handful of cilantro leaves

Preheat your oven to 350°F (180°C) and warm the taco shells on a plate for a few minutes while you prepare the bacon and eggs.

Place your favourite heavy frying pan over medium-high heat and toss in the bacon. Cook, stirring frequently, until brown and crisp. While the bacon is browning, thoroughly whisk the eggs and Cheddar together. Season them with salt and pepper to your taste.

When the bacon is crisp, remove it from the pan with a slotted spoon and drain it on a folded paper towel. Pour off about half of the bacon fat and return the pan to medium heat. Pour the eggs into the pan and patiently scramble them, stirring constantly with a wooden spoon or rubber spatula, until they're cooked through but still creamy, 2 or 3 minutes.

Spoon the eggs into the warm taco shells. Top with a spoonful of salsa, the crisp bacon, green onion, and a few cilantro leaves. Serve and share!

KITCHEN TIP

- If you frequently cook bacon, keep a metal can in your refrigerator to pour the leftover fat into. It's easier to toss out when it's solid.
- Cut the lid off an egg carton and use the slotted bottom to help stuff and serve the tacos.

POTATO BACON CHEDDAR BREAKFAST BAKE

This classic group of flavours tastes great no matter how they show up at the table or even what time they get there. In this version, crisp bacon, browned potatoes, and tangy Cheddar are baked together with simple eggs. A true breakfast treat that's just as flavourful at brunch, lunch, or dinner—especially with a simple green salad. **Serves 4**

8 slices of bacon, cut into chunks
1 large baking potato, unpeeled
8 eggs
2 green onions, sliced
1 tablespoon (15 mL) of chopped fresh thyme, or 1 teaspoon (5 mL) dried
1 heaping cup (275 mL) of grated Cheddar cheese
A pinch or two of salt and lots of freshly ground pepper
4 garlic cloves, thinly sliced

Preheat your oven to 400°F (200°C).

Place a large nonstick frying pan over medium-high heat and toss in the bacon. Cook, stirring frequently, until it's brown and crisp. While the bacon is browning, give the potato a good rinse. Dry it off, then cut it into 16 chunks. When the bacon is crisp, remove it from the pan with a slotted spoon, leaving the sizzling, flavourful fat behind. Drain the bacon on a folded paper towel.

Gently ease the potatoes into the sizzling bacon fat. Patiently pan-fry them, stirring frequently, until they are cooked through and lightly browned, 5 to 10 minutes. Meanwhile, whisk together the eggs, green onions, thyme, and half of the cheese. Season the mixture to your taste with salt and pepper.

When the potatoes are brown, pour off most of the bacon fat. Lower the heat and stir in the garlic. Continue stirring for a few moments until everything is fragrant. Remove the pan from the heat. Pour in the eggs, toss in the crisp bacon, and stir everything together. Sprinkle with the remaining cheese and bake until fully firm, 15 to 20 minutes.

If you've used a nonstick pan, gently loosen the edges with a rubber spatula, then slide gently onto a serving platter. For conventional pans, simply scoop and share. If you need to buy some time, return the pan to the oven, turn the oven off, and keep it warm for an hour or so. You may also cover the pan loosely with a kitchen towel and rest it on your counter until it's time to serve.

KITCHEN TIP

Frying potatoes in any fat or oil is an excellent way to deliciously brown them. For best results, adjust the heat as high as possible, but not so high that the fat begins to burn and smoke. Not too low either, or the potatoes won't heat up enough to brown. Fiddle with the temperature a bit and you'll soon find the sweet spot. The potatoes will sizzle dramatically, but just keep an eye on them—you'll know which way to adjust the heat.

SMOKED SALMON QUICHE WITH GRUYÈRE AND DILL

Smoked salmon is a classic A.M. treat, especially when it's baked into this extravagant quiche with a few familiar flavours. Dill's aromatic brightness and the rich nuttiness of Gruyère complement the smooth richness of the smoked salmon. This is a weekend treat! **Serves 6 to 8**

1 sheet of frozen puff pastry (half a 411 g package)
6 eggs
2 cups (500 mL) of sour cream
1 cup (250 mL) of chopped fresh dill, including tender stems
2 green onions, sliced
1/2 teaspoon (2 mL) of salt
1/2 teaspoon (2 mL) of freshly ground pepper
8 ounces (250 g) or more of your favourite smoked salmon, pre-sliced
1 cup (250 mL) of grated Gruyère cheese

Place a pizza stone or baking sheet in the middle of your oven and preheat it to 375°F (190°C). Either will help transfer the oven's heat to the pastry shell. Lightly oil an 8-inch (20 cm) wide, 2-inch (5 cm) deep fluted tart pan with a removable bottom or a 9-inch (23 cm) ceramic quiche dish, pie pan, or other baking pan.

Lightly dust your work surface and rolling pin with flour. Lightly dust both sides of the frozen pastry with more flour. Let it rest to thaw for a few minutes until it softens. Roll the pastry into a rounded square about 12 inches (30 cm) across. Fit it into your baking pan. Trim the edges, leaving an inch or so to roll into a crusty rim, or simply roll your rolling pin across the edge for a sleeker look. Prick the bottom evenly with a fork to prevent it from rising while it cooks. Bake the empty shell on the preheated stone or baking sheet until it's lightly browned, 15 to 20 minutes or so.

Crack the eggs into a medium bowl and whisk them well. Add the sour cream, dill, green onions, salt, and pepper and whisk until smooth. Layer the smoked salmon slices on top of each other and slice into broad ribbons. Gently stir them into the eggs. Pour the filling into the baked pastry shell. Evenly sprinkle the Gruyère over the surface. Bake the quiche until the centre sets, about 45 minutes.

Serve the quiche straight out of the oven or keep it warm by turning off the oven and leaving the quiche in for an hour or so. You may also cool it on your counter for a while, loosely covered with a kitchen towel. If you used a tart pan, remove the rim before you share your masterpiece.

KITCHEN TIP

The stems of many fresh herbs are as tender and flavourful as the delicate leaves. They're easily chopped, measured, and stirred into your cooking. Parsley, basil, sage, and dill stems are tender. Rosemary, tarragon, and thyme stems are too tough, though.

APPLE PIE PANCAKES WITH CARAMEL SYRUP

Stirring grated apple and cinnamon into my standard whole grain pancakes upgrades this breakfast staple into an A.M. treat. The recipe can easily be doubled. **Serves 4**

FOR THE CARAMEL SYRUP

1 cup (250 mL) of sugar

FOR THE PANCAKES

1 cup (250 mL) of all-purpose flour
1 cup (250 mL) of whole wheat flour
1 cup (250 mL) of any kind of rolled oats
2 tablespoons (30 mL) of baking powder
1 tablespoon (15 mL) of cinnamon
1/2 teaspoon (2 mL) of salt
2 eggs
1-1/2 cups (375 mL) of milk (cow's, rice, or soy)
1/4 cup (60 mL) of melted butter
2 tablespoons (30 mL) of brown sugar
1 teaspoon (5 mL) of vanilla
3 cups (750 mL) of grated local apples
A splash of vegetable oil

To make the caramel syrup, pour 1 cup (250 mL) of water into a small saucepan over medium-high heat. Sprinkle in the sugar, evenly distributing it over the water and taking care to avoid the inside edge of the pan. Simmer the mixture, without stirring, until the water evaporates and leaves behind pure sugar syrup. The temperature will rise, and in a few minutes the syrup will begin to lightly brown. Swirl the pan gently and continue cooking until the syrup is golden brown and fragrant. Carefully pour in 1/4 cup (60 mL) of water to stop the cooking. It will sputter and sizzle. Continue heating, stirring until the water and caramel dissolve into caramel syrup. Pour into a jar and refrigerate until cool and thickened.

Preheat your largest frying pan over medium-high heat. Meanwhile, in a large bowl, whisk together the all-purpose flour, whole wheat flour, oats, baking powder, cinnamon, and salt, evenly distributing the finer powders among the coarser ones. In a second bowl, whisk together the eggs, milk, butter, sugar, and vanilla. Stir in the grated apples, then pour the wet mixture into the dry one. Stir with a wooden spoon just until a smooth batter forms.

Pour a splash of vegetable oil into your hot pan and swirl the pan to evenly coat the bottom with a thin film. Spoon the batter into the pan, forming your choice of large or small pancakes. Cook, turning once, until deliciously golden brown on each side, about 5 minutes in total. Serve with the caramel syrup.

KITCHEN TIP

The key to great pancakes is the right pan temperature—high enough to brown the outside but not so high that the exterior burns before the inside finishes cooking. Your preheated pan is at the perfect temperature when water drops dance on it without immediately evaporating (too hot) or just sitting and simmering (too cool).

CARAMEL APPLE "FLIPJACK"

There are few flavours as addictive as caramelized apples, especially as one of the first tastes of the day. This spectacular dish is an A.M. showstopper that's so easy to make you'll impress yourself in your own kitchen before impressing everyone at your table! **Serves 6 or so**

2 tablespoons (30 mL) of butter
1 cup (250 mL) of white sugar
2 large unpeeled local apples
1 cup (250 mL) of all-purpose flour
1 cup (250 mL) of whole wheat flour
1 cup (250 mL) of any kind of rolled oats
2 tablespoons (30 mL) of baking powder
1 teaspoon (5 mL) of nutmeg
1/2 teaspoon (2 mL) of salt
2 eggs
1-1/2 cups (375 mL) of milk (cow's, rice, or soy)
1/4 cup (60 mL) of vegetable oil
2 tablespoons (30 mL) of brown sugar
1 teaspoon (5 mL) of vanilla

Preheat your oven to 350°F (190°C).

Melt the butter in your favourite frying pan over medium-high heat. Gently swirl the pan to evenly coat the bottom, then sprinkle the white sugar over the butter. Continue heating, gently swirling a bit, until the sugar becomes golden brown and fragrant, about 5 minutes. Remove from the heat.

Core the apples and slice each one into 8 wedges. Arrange the wedges cut side down on the caramel to form an attractive outer ring, overlapping as needed, then filling the inside.

In a large bowl, whisk together the all-purpose flour, whole wheat flour, oats, baking powder, nutmeg, and salt, evenly distributing the finer powders among the coarser ones. In a second bowl, whisk together the eggs, milk, oil, brown sugar, and vanilla. Pour the wet mixture into the dry one. Stir with a wooden spoon just until a smooth batter forms. Carefully pour the batter over the apples. Bake until firm and cooked through, 20 to 30 minutes.

Gently loosen the sides with a rubber spatula, then cover with a large serving plate. Carefully invert the works, remove the pan, and reveal your masterpiece. If there is any caramel left in the pan, reheat it over medium heat until you can drizzle it over the flipjack. Serve and share!

KITCHEN TIP

Quick batters like this one are at their best when they're barely mixed. Too much mixing encourages the gluten in the flour to toughen, as it does in bread doughs. Instead, a quick, efficient mixing doesn't overwork the flour, allowing the batter to stay tender as it bakes.

FRENCH TOAST SANDWICHES OATMEAL CRUSTED WITH BLUEBERRY STUFFING AND MARMALADE MINT BUTTER

It's easy to add a few Saturday morning flourishes to a pan full of butter-fried French toast. Thick slices of hearty bread, cream cheese blueberry stuffing, a simple egg batter for dipping, an oat crust, and marmalade butter all add up to an excellent opportunity to score some major breakfast-in-bed brownie points. **Serves 4**

4 ounces (125 g) of softened cream cheese

1 heaping cup (275 mL) of fresh or frozen wild blueberries

2 tablespoons (30 mL) of maple syrup

8 thick slices of whole-grain bread

4 eggs

1 cup (250 mL) of milk

2 tablespoons (30 mL) of brown sugar

1 teaspoon (5 mL) of vanilla

1/2 teaspoon (2 mL) of nutmeg

2 cups (500 mL) of quick-cooking rolled oats

2 tablespoons (30 mL) of butter

FOR THE MARMALADE BUTTER

1/2 cup (125 mL) of softened butter

1/4 cup (60 mL) of orange marmalade

1/4 cup (60 mL) of thinly sliced fresh mint leaves

Stir together the cream cheese, blueberries, and maple syrup. Evenly spread the filling onto 4 of the bread slices. Form sandwiches with the remaining 4 slices, gently pressing them so they stick together. Put the sandwiches in a container that they fit in snugly, either stacked or side by side. Whisk together the eggs, milk, brown sugar, vanilla, and nutmeg. Pour the mixture over the sandwiches, lifting and turning them to maximize their absorption. Soak the sandwiches, turning them now and then, until they're saturated, about 10 minutes.

Preheat your oven to 400°F (200°C).

Pour the oats into a shallow pan. Once the sandwiches have absorbed all the egg batter, dredge them in the oats, turning them to evenly coat each side. Set them aside as you ready the frying pan.

Melt the butter in your favourite large frying pan over medium-high heat until it begins to foam and lightly brown. Immediately add the sandwiches and gently pan-fry them, turning once, until they're golden brown on both sides. Listen, and adjust the heat so the butter continues to sizzle. When they've browned nicely, place them on a baking sheet and bake until heated through and evenly cooked, another 5 minutes or so.

Meanwhile, to make the marmalade butter, stir together the softened butter, marmalade, and mint. Serve the French toast with the marmalade butter and lots of maple syrup.

KITCHEN TIP

Bread's ability to absorb aromatic egg batter defines French toast. The moisture in the batter softens the texture of the bread. Along the way the bread absorbs the flavours of vanilla and nutmeg from the batter. The eggs and surface moisture help the oats adhere. Finally, when the batter cooks through, the natural binding ability of the eggs transforms the bread's texture to custard.

BUTTERMILK WAFFLES WITH CINNAMON APPLE STEW

The nooks and crannies of these tangy buttermilk-flavoured waffles easily absorb the tasty juices of a simple apple stew. The butter batter doesn't stick to the waffle iron and gives the waffles their memorable rich flavour and crisp texture. **Serves 4**

FOR THE APPLE STEW

2 or 3 of your favourite apples, unpeeled, cored, and chopped into small chunks
1 cup (250 mL) of cider or apple juice
1/4 cup (60 mL) of brown sugar
2 teaspoons (10 mL) of cinnamon

FOR THE WAFFLES

3 cups (750 mL) of all-purpose flour
1 tablespoon (15 mL) of baking powder
1 teaspoon (5 mL) of baking soda
1 teaspoon (5 mL) of nutmeg
1/2 teaspoon (2 mL) of salt
3 eggs
3 cups (750 mL) of well-shaken buttermilk
1 cup (250 mL) of butter (2 sticks), melted and cooled

To make the apple stew, put the apples into a small saucepan and add the cider, brown sugar, and cinnamon. Bring the mixture to a simmer over medium heat. Stir frequently and continue to cook as the apples soften and the mixture thickens, about 10 minutes. Remove from the heat and set aside for serving.

Preheat your waffle iron. In a large bowl, whisk together the flour, baking powder, baking soda, nutmeg, and salt, evenly distributing the finer powders among the coarser ones. In a separate bowl, whisk together the eggs, buttermilk, and melted butter. Pour the wet mixture into the dry ingredients. Quickly stir everything together, forming a smooth, thick batter.

Lightly oil your waffle iron. Spoon in enough batter to cover about half of the cooking surface, allowing lots of room for expansion. Cook for about 5 minutes. You'll know the waffles are nearly done when steam stops escaping around the edges. If you feel any resistance when you try to lift the lid, give them another minute or so to finish cooking. Serve and share with the warm apple stew.

KITCHEN TIP

This batter includes both baking powder and baking soda. Here's why. Baking powder contains baking soda. Baking soda must be activated by combining it with something acidic, like sour buttermilk, which triggers the leavening effect of the soda. But there's not enough tanginess in the buttermilk to fully lift the waffles. That's why baking powder is helpful. It contains both baking soda and a mildly acidic powder as a built-in catalyst. It picks up where the baking soda leaves off and leavens all by itself.

EXTRA-BLUEBERRY MUFFINS WITH BROWN BUTTER

My mom has baked me thousands of blueberry muffins, and all of them inspire this recipe. We'd pick and freeze blueberries all summer long, and she'd cram as many as possible into every muffin she baked. These muffins maximize blueberries per bite. She didn't serve them with brown butter, but I do. It's the only way I can think of to improve them! **Makes 12 muffins**

2-1/2 cups (625 mL) of all-purpose flour
2 tablespoons (30 mL) of baking powder
2 teaspoons (10 mL) of nutmeg
1/2 teaspoon (2 mL) of salt
4 eggs

1 cup (250 mL) of brown sugar
1 cup (250 mL) of milk
1 cup (250 mL) of melted butter
1 tablespoon (15 mL) of vanilla
2 cups (500 mL) of fresh or frozen blueberries
1/4 cup (60 mL) of coarse sugar

Preheat your oven to 400°F (200°C). Lightly oil the cups and top surface of a standard 12-muffin pan.

In a large bowl, whisk together the flour, baking powder, nutmeg, and salt, evenly distributing the finer powders among the coarser ones. In a separate bowl, whisk together the eggs, brown sugar, milk, butter, and vanilla. Pour the wet mixture into the dry mixture. Stir together with a few quick strokes just until a slightly lumpy batter forms, about 20 seconds. Pour in the berries and gently stir them in with just a few more quick strokes. Portion the batter into the muffin cups. Evenly coat the top of each one with a sprinkling of coarse sugar.

Bake for 20 to 25 minutes or so, until the muffins are golden brown and a toothpick inserted into several of them comes out clean. Rest on a rack for a few minutes before turning them out of the pan. Muffins are at their best freshly baked, so serve and share immediately. For an extra-special treat serve with the following brown butter.

KITCHEN TIP

Muffins are best tender. Bread the opposite. The difference lies in how the flour is treated. Kneading bread dough develops gluten and builds strength, but if you develop that same gluten in muffin batter, you'll end up with tough little pucks. Beating a batter to the point of smoothness develops the strong gluten in flour, toughening and coarsening the muffins, leaving them full of holes. Batter gently and smoothly mixed, merely moistened with just a few strokes, stays tender. The melted butter doesn't hurt either, as it interferes with gluten formation.

BROWN BUTTER

When butter is melted, the small amount of water it contains boils away. With the water gone, the remaining purer fat heats to a higher temperature. Eventually the small amount of milkfat solids it contains brown and caramelize, creating a deeply satisfying new nutty flavour. Cool it, then whip into more butter for an addictive topping for these muffins, or for French toast, pancakes, toast, or any other baked treat. **Makes about 1 cup (250 mL)**

1 cup (250 mL) of softened butter (2 sticks)

Put half of the butter into a small pan over medium heat. Swirl gently as it melts and begins to foam. Eventually the foam will begin to subside and you'll notice sediment browning in the bottom of the pan. Continue swirling until the sediment becomes deep golden brown. Immediately pour the butter and all of the flavourful sediment into a shallow bowl. Rest, swirling occasionally, until cooled to room temperature. This will take at least an hour, so it's best done well in advance, even the day before. The brown butter may safely rest overnight, covered, at room temperature.

Once the brown butter has cooled, toss the remaining softened butter into a small bowl and whisk it by hand (or use an electric mixer). Add the cooled brown butter and sediment a bit at a time, whisking constantly until they are thoroughly mixed. Transfer to a small serving bowl. (This butter may be made several days ahead and kept at room temperature until needed.)

VANILLA YOGURT MUESLI WITH TEN FRUITS, NUTS, AND SEEDS

When I cooked for the athletes of the world at the 2010 Vancouver Olympic Games, this muesli was my essential start to every day. It's packed full of nutrition and get-your-day-started flavour. Maybe that's why we served 100 pounds of it every day! **Serves 4 to 6**

2 cups (500 mL) of large-flake rolled oats
1/4 cup (60 mL) of thinly sliced dried apricots
1 cup (250 mL) of vanilla yogurt
1 cup (250 mL) of apple juice
1/4 cup (60 mL) of honey
1 teaspoon (5 mL) of vanilla
1 apple, coarsely grated on a box grater
1/2 cup (125 mL) of your favourite berries, fresh or frozen
1/4 cup (60 mL) of moist raisins
1/4 cup (60 mL) of almond slivers
1/4 cup (60 mL) of walnut pieces
1/4 cup (60 mL) of sunflower seeds
1/4 cup (60 mL) of pumpkin seeds
1/4 cup (60 mL) of shredded sweetened coconut

In a large bowl, stir the oats and apricots together first to help separate the sticky apricot pieces from each other. Toss in everything else and stir together. Refrigerate for an hour or so to give the oats time to absorb the surrounding liquid and soften up. Serve and share!

KITCHEN TIP

It's easy to simply stir muesli together every night so it will soften and be ready for breakfast. Muesli is also easily made in larger batches and kept refrigerated for several days. Every day just stir it smooth before serving.

SANDWICHES

Old-School Italian Sub with Marinated Peppers and Arugula, 27

Sausage and Pepper Hero with Lots of Fennel Seeds, 28

Garlic-Rubbed Crostini with Mediterranean Tuna Salad, 31

Shrimp Rice Paper Rolls with Ginger Peanut Sauce and Cilantro, 32

Chicken Cheddar Quesadillas with Jalapeño Cilantro Pesto, 37

BLT and A: Bacon, Lettuce, Tomato, and Grilled Avocado Sandwich, 38

Grilled Pizza with Garlic and Thyme-Scented Olive Oil, Tomatoes, and Mozzarella, 41

Lamb Pita Burgers with Cinnamon Mint Ketchup, 42

Bill's Crispy Chewy Double Taco, 45

Hot and Cold Olympic Club Sandwich, 46

OLD-SCHOOL ITALIAN SUB WITH MARINATED PEPPERS AND ARUGULA

This is my version of the classic spicy sandwich found in mom-and-pop delis all over North America. For best results, source the very best quality meats and cheese you can. A good deli will also carry peperoncini, cherry peppers, and crusty Italian bread, everything you need for a halftime break or a summer supper. This is a sandwich for a crowd. **Serves 6 to 8**

1/2 cup (125 mL) of extra virgin olive oil
1/4 cup (60 mL) of red wine vinegar
1 tablespoon (15 mL) of Dijon mustard
1 teaspoon (5 mL) of dried oregano
2 garlic cloves, minced
1 cup (250 mL) of chopped fresh Italian parsley
A pinch or two of salt
1 red onion, thinly sliced
1/2 cup (125 mL) of seeded and chopped peperoncini or banana peppers
1/2 cup (125 mL) of seeded and chopped cherry peppers
1 large loaf of Italian bread, about 24 inches (60 cm) long
2 handfuls of arugula
4 large ripe tomatoes, sliced
8 ounces (250 g) each of thinly sliced authentic capocollo, mortadella, and salami
4 ounces (125 g) of thinly sliced prosciutto
6 ounces (175 g) of thinly sliced provolone cheese

Whisk together the olive oil, vinegar, mustard, oregano, garlic, and parsley until they form a smooth dressing. Season with salt to your taste. Throw in the onion and peppers, tossing them until they're coated with the dressing. Rest for an hour or so, giving the flavours time to fully develop.

When the onion and peppers have marinated, begin building the sandwich. Cut the bread in half lengthwise. Spread the pepper mixture evenly over both halves. Layer the arugula and tomatoes on the bottom half. Evenly layer the meats one at a time over the tomatoes, then top with the cheese. Cover with the top half of the bread. Skewer with a series of picks. Using a serrated knife, slice into 4-inch (10 cm) sections. Serve and share!

KITCHEN TIP

This sandwich may be made in advance and sliced just before serving. Giving it time to rest allows the juicy marinated onions and peppers to soak into the bread and permeate the sandwich with their aromatic flavour.

SAUSAGE AND PEPPER HERO WITH LOTS OF FENNEL SEEDS

Nothing beats a warm hero bun stuffed with hot-from-the-grill Italian sausages topped with peppers and onions. For an extra flavour burst, this recipe includes a generous dose of fennel seeds, the same seasoning that gives Italian sausage its distinctive flavour. **Serves 4**

2 tablespoons (30 mL) of olive oil
1 large onion, thinly sliced
1 tablespoon (15 mL) of fennel seeds
1 red bell pepper, seeded and thinly sliced
1 green bell pepper, seeded and thinly sliced
1 yellow bell pepper, seeded and thinly sliced
A sprinkle or two of salt and lots of freshly ground pepper
4 Italian sausages
4 hero rolls

Prepare and preheat your grill to its highest setting.

Splash the olive oil into your favourite sauté pan or heavy frying pan over medium-high heat. When it's hot, add the onion and cook, stirring frequently, until it becomes golden brown, about 10 minutes. Add the fennel seeds and peppers and continue cooking just long enough for the peppers to soften. Season with salt and pepper to your taste. Reserve until you're ready to assemble the heroes.

Grill the sausages until they're cooked through and juicy, about 10 minutes. As they cook, gently slice open the hero rolls with a serrated knife, leaving a hinge so they lie flat like a book. Lightly brush the cut sides with olive oil and grill until lightly toasted and heated through.

Stuff each hero roll with a sausage and top with lots of the peppers and onions. Serve and share!

KITCHEN TIP

Toasting the hero rolls does several things for the bread. The heat of the grill removes any shelf staleness while adding the golden brown flavour and crisp crunchiness of toasting.

GARLIC-RUBBED CROSTINI WITH MEDITERRANEAN TUNA SALAD

These crostini are perfect for a crispy, tasty snack, side dish, or party hors d'oeuvre. You'll be amazed at how much flavour you can add to a slice of toasted baguette by simply rubbing it with raw garlic. That pungent aroma is the perfect base for a simple tuna salad dressed up with a few classic Mediterranean flavours. **Serves 6 to 8**

FOR THE CROSTINI

1 baguette, cut diagonally into 16 or so 1/2-inch (1 cm) thick slices
1/4 cup (60 mL) of extra virgin olive oil
Freshly ground black pepper
1 garlic clove, cut in half lengthwise

FOR THE TUNA SALAD

The zest and juice of 1 lemon
2 tablespoons (30 mL) of extra virgin olive oil
1 tablespoon (15 mL) of Dijon mustard
2 cans (each 6-1/2 ounces/184 g) of tuna
2 green onions, thinly sliced
1/2 cup (125 mL) of chopped pitted Kalamata olives
1 tablespoon (15 mL) of drained capers
A pinch or two of salt and lots of freshly ground pepper
12 large fresh basil leaves

Preheat your oven to 400°F (200°C).

To make the crostini, arrange the baguette slices on a baking sheet. Lightly brush each one with olive oil. Season with pepper to your taste. Bake, turning the tray once, until golden brown and toasted, about 10 minutes. Remove from the oven and rub each crostini vigorously with the cut side of the garlic clove.

To make the tuna salad, whisk together the lemon zest, lemon juice, oil, and mustard. Add the tuna, juice and all, breaking it into flakes with a fork. Toss in the green onions, olives, and capers. Season with salt and pepper to your taste. Toss everything together. Spoon the mixture onto the crisp crostini. Stack the basil leaves with the biggest leaves on the bottom, then roll them into a tight cigar shape. Slice into thin threads and sprinkle them over the crostini. Serve and share!

KITCHEN TIP

One of the keys to great crostini is taking the time to thoroughly brown them. They're at their best when they're entirely golden brown—not just along the edges. Your patience will be rewarded with lots of toasted flavour and a crispy base that's easy to hold.

SHRIMP RICE PAPER ROLLS WITH GINGER PEANUT SAUCE AND CILANTRO

Wrapping flavourful foods in rice paper rounds is a great kitchen trick to have up your sleeve. Crisp at first, the rounds quickly soften in water, becoming an easily rolled flavour wrapper. Here they transform an Asian-inspired shrimp salad into a flavourful treat. **Makes 8 rolls**

The zest and juice of 1 lime
1 tablespoon (15 mL) of grated frozen ginger
1 tablespoon (15 mL) of peanut butter
1 tablespoon (15 mL) of soy sauce
1 tablespoon (15 mL) of honey
1 tablespoon (15 mL) of rice wine vinegar
1/4 teaspoon (1 mL) of your favourite hot sauce
8 ounces (250 g) of cooked peeled deveined shrimp, chopped

1/4 cup (60 mL) of roasted peanuts, coarsely chopped
2 cups (500 mL) or so of bean sprouts
1 carrot, coarsely grated on a box grater
1 red onion, thinly sliced
20 snow peas, thinly sliced
8 rice paper rounds (8-1/2 inches/21 cm)
A handful of cilantro leaves

In a medium bowl, whisk together the lime zest and juice, ginger, peanut butter, soy sauce, honey, rice wine vinegar, and hot sauce. Add the shrimp, peanuts, bean sprouts, carrot, onion, and snow peas. Toss until the dressing coats the salad.

Lay an absorbent kitchen towel on your work surface. Fill a pie plate with warm water. Slip in a rice paper sheet and let it soak until soft and pliable, about 45 seconds. Carefully remove it with your fingers, gently stretching out the circle in the air so it can drip dry for a few moments. Lay the circle out on the towel.

Centre 6 or 8 cilantro leaves on the rice paper in two tight lines just above the middle, staying 2 inches (5 cm) or so away from the sides. Neatly position a compact log-shaped mound of one-eighth of the shrimp filling next to the cilantro leaves, about 2 inches (5 cm) from the bottom edge and 2 inches from the sides. Fold the bottom of the rice paper over the filling, rolling and tightening until it snugly encloses the salad. Fold in the sides, slightly angling them inward, then gently roll the works into as tight a cylinder as possible. Lay the roll seam side down on a serving platter and repeat with the remaining rice paper rounds.

Serve the shrimp rolls immediately or cover them with a barely damp paper towel or plastic wrap and refrigerate for a few hours.

KITCHEN TIP

- Frozen ginger is easily grated into a fine powder on a microplane grater.
- Your first couple of rice paper rolls may be a bit wobbly but you'll quickly get the hang of rolling them tightly. It's helpful to fold in the sides as tightly as you can, forming the salad into a tight cylinder. Slightly angling the edges inward means you won't be left with sloppy overhanging edges.

SALT & PEPPER

"Season to your taste with a sprinkle or two of salt and lots of freshly ground pepper." Every recipe includes these instructions, but what do they really mean?

Salt makes our food taste better; it enhances other flavours. But too much salt is ruinous to our health, so fortunately a little bit goes a long way. Over time, though, we can become desensitized to its presence and may need more to get the previous flavouring effect. Instead, try using a little less every time you cook, gradually lowering your tolerance. Season to your evolving taste!

Pepper is much more than just spicy heat. Freshly ground pepper is packed with intense aromatic flavour that pleasingly perfumes your cooking. That flavour diminishes quickly after grinding, though.

CHICKEN CHEDDAR QUESADILLAS WITH JALAPEÑO CILANTRO PESTO

Quesadillas are an easy way to get a lot of flavour on the table in a hurry. I love making them with this incredibly aromatic pesto. It's packed with bright cilantro, smooth almonds, and spicy jalapeño. For this memorable treat, spread it on tortillas, then layer and bake them with grilled chicken strips and lots of Cheddar cheese. **Serves 4**

1 large bunch of cilantro, stems and all
1 cup (250 mL) of unsalted roasted almonds
1/4 cup (60 mL) of olive oil
The zest and juice of 2 limes
1 jalapeño
8 flour tortillas (6 inch/15 cm)
Vegetable oil for brushing the tortillas
2 large grilled chicken breasts, thinly sliced
2 green onions, thinly sliced
1 cup (250 mL) of grated Cheddar or Monterey Jack cheese
1 cup (250 mL) of sour cream

Preheat your oven to 450°F (230°C).

Toss the cilantro, almonds, olive oil, lime zest and juice, and jalapeño into your food processor and process into a thick paste. If necessary, thin the pesto to an easily spreadable consistency with a splash or two of water.

Lightly brush the top of 4 of the tortillas with vegetable oil and place them oiled side down on a baking sheet. Set aside 1 tablespoon (15 mL) of the pesto, and spread the remaining pesto evenly over the tortillas. Cover with a layer of chicken slices. Sprinkle with the green onions and cheese. Cover with the remaining tortillas and lightly brush the top of each one with vegetable oil.

Bake the quesadillas until the cheese melts and the tortillas are browned and crispy, about 10 minutes. Meanwhile, stir the reserved pesto into the sour cream. Cut the quesadillas into quarters and serve and share with the sour cream dip.

KITCHEN TIP
I like to spend time to save time. Every now and then I fire up my grill and fill it with searing chicken breasts. They're easily frozen and offer a quick and easy way to pull together a meal in a hurry, especially in a batch of these simple spicy quesadillas.

BLT AND A: BACON, LETTUCE, TOMATO, AND GRILLED AVOCADO SANDWICH

This is my favourite sandwich. I didn't think it was possible to improve upon the classic BLT until I tried grilling a few avocado halves and layering them on. It's amazing how easy it is to grill avocados. With grilled bread, this humble sandwich is an instant classic. **Serves 4**

12 slices of the best available thick-cut bacon
2 ripe avocados
Olive oil for brushing
A pinch or two of salt and lots of freshly ground pepper
8 thick slices of whole-grain bread
1/2 cup (125 mL) of mayonnaise
4 large leaves of leaf lettuce
2 or 3 large ripe local tomatoes, thinly sliced

Prepare and preheat your grill to its highest setting.

In a heavy frying pan over medium-high heat, cook the bacon until it's crisp. Drain on a few folded paper towels.

Halve the avocados and remove their pits. Using a large spoon, scoop the flesh out of each skin in one piece. Gently press the avocado halves down on a plate, flattening them slightly and splitting them a bit. Lightly brush them with olive oil and season them to your taste with salt and pepper. Lightly coat both sides of the bread slices with a bit of mayonnaise.

Lightly oil the grill grates, then add the avocado halves and bread slices. Grill the avocados just long enough to heat them through, 2 or 3 minutes per side. Turn the bread slices once or twice until they're lightly toasted and smoky on both sides.

Layer the lettuce and tomatoes on 4 slices of the toast. Season the tomatoes with salt and pepper to your taste. Top with the bacon, grilled avocado, and remaining bread slices. Serve and share!

KITCHEN TIP
It's a bit unconventional to brush mayonnaise on bread before grilling it, but it works. The oil in the sweet mayonnaise helps the bread toast. The results are crispy and delicious.

GRILLED PIZZA WITH GARLIC AND THYME-SCENTED OLIVE OIL, TOMATOES, AND MOZZARELLA

Grilling pizza is a revelation. The results are rustically authentic, wonderfully smoky, simultaneously chewy yet crisp, and so delicious that they'll forever change the way you think about pizza. Like any pizza, it's best not to load the dough down with too many elaborate toppings, though. When grilling, it's easier to handle several smaller pizzas than one or two large ones. **Makes 4 pizzas, serving 4 to 8**

2 bags of store-bought pizza dough, thawed if frozen
1/2 cup (125 mL) of olive oil, plus a splash or two more for brushing
4 garlic cloves, minced
1 tablespoon (15 mL) of minced fresh thyme
4 large ripe tomatoes, thinly sliced
A pinch or two of salt and lots of freshly ground pepper
4 balls of fresh buffalo mozzarella cheese

An hour or so before you're ready to bake the pizzas, remove the dough from the refrigerator. Divide each ball in half, dust with flour, and shape into 4 balls. Rest the dough on the counter, loosely covered with a kitchen towel. It will relax and rise.

Meanwhile, pour 1/2 cup (125 mL) of the olive oil into a small saucepan over medium heat. Add the garlic and gently cook until the oil is sizzling and the scent of garlic fills your kitchen, a minute or so. Remove from the heat and stir in the thyme.

Prepare and preheat your grill to its highest setting.

Lightly dust your work surface, the dough balls, a rolling pin, and your hands with flour. Quickly and firmly roll out each ball into a thin, roughly round pizza base. They don't need to be perfectly round, and have much more personality when they're a bit unevenly shaped.

Lightly oil the grill grates. Brush the top of each pizza base with a bit of plain olive oil, then carefully flip 2 of them onto the grates. Grill until the top puffs up a bit and the bottoms crisp, about 3 minutes. With a pair of tongs, flip them over and grill for just another minute or two.

Remove the pizzas from the grill. Onto each pizza, spoon one-quarter of the garlic-scented olive oil, evenly spreading it within an inch or so of the edges. Add an even layer of a quarter of the tomato slices, covering as much of the surface as possible without overlapping them. Season them to your taste with salt and pepper. Crumble a quarter of the mozzarella cheese onto the tomato slices. Return the pizzas to the grill, close the lid, and grill until the bottom browns and the cheese melts, another 3 minutes or so. Transfer to a cutting board, cut into wedges, serve, and share!

KITCHEN TIP
Once you've tried grilling pizza, you'll realize how easy it is to use your favourite sauce or toppings on the grill. Anything goes!

LAMB PITA BURGERS
WITH CINNAMON MINT KETCHUP

Who says burgers can only be made with ground beef or that you have to buy ketchup at the store? Not me! Ground lamb makes a tasty burger that easily absorbs lots of Mediterranean flavour. Top with your own homemade ketchup and you'll forget all about beef burgers. **Serves 4**

FOR THE KETCHUP

1 can (28 ounces/796 mL) of whole tomatoes
8 garlic cloves, chopped
1/2 cup (125 mL) of red wine vinegar
1/4 cup (60 mL) of sugar
1 tablespoon (15 mL) of cinnamon
1 teaspoon (5 mL) of salt
1 teaspoon (5 mL) of your favourite hot sauce
1 cup (250 mL) of chopped fresh mint

FOR THE BURGERS

1-1/2 pounds (750 g) of ground lamb
1 cup (250 mL) of minced onion
2 garlic cloves, minced
1 tablespoon (15 mL) of ground cumin
1 teaspoon (5 mL) of salt
Freshly ground pepper
4 small whole wheat pitas
4 lettuce leaves, rolled tightly and sliced into shreds

Begin by making the ketchup. Pour the tomatoes and their juice into a large saucepan, then mash them with a fork into smaller chunks. Add the garlic, vinegar, sugar, cinnamon, salt, and hot sauce. Bring the mixture to a boil, then reduce the heat so the mixture is just barely simmering. Continue cooking, uncovered and stirring occasionally, until the mixture reduces to a thick, chunky paste, 30 to 40 minutes. Remove from the heat, stir in the mint, and refrigerate to thicken further. (You can make this ketchup several days in advance, and it will keep for several weeks in your refrigerator.)

Prepare and preheat your grill to its highest setting.

Put the lamb, onion, garlic, and cumin in a bowl. Season to taste with salt and pepper. With clean hands, quickly mix everything together, then form into 4 evenly shaped burgers about 1 inch (2.5 cm) thick. Grill the burgers until they're medium, 5 to 7 minutes per side.

Slice the top inch or so off the pitas, then gently coax them open and place a burger inside each one. Add a tangle of shredded lettuce and a spoonful of homemade ketchup. Serve and share!

KITCHEN TIP

The key to a perfect burger—lamb or beef—is freshly ground meat, minimally handled. Overmixing the meat overworks and toughens it. That's why hands work best: they'll always be more efficient than any other kitchen tool.

BILL'S CRISPY CHEWY DOUBLE TACO

Love brightly flavoured tacos but don't like the way the crisp shell always breaks and make a mess in your hand? My chef buddy Bill Pratt showed me the solution. Fill a standard crisp corn taco first, then nestle it in a small soft flour taco, thus containing the mess when the crisp shell inevitably breaks. I liked the idea so much that Bill and I served thousands of these tacos in the Whistler Athletes' Village during the 2010 Winter Olympics. **Serves 4**

FOR THE FILLING

2 tablespoons (30 mL) of vegetable oil

1 pound (500 g) of ground beef

1 onion, chopped

4 garlic cloves, minced

2 tablespoons (30 mL) of chili powder

1 tablespoon (15 mL) of cumin

1 tablespoon (15 mL) of dried oregano

1 large ripe tomato, diced

2 tablespoons (30 mL) of ketchup

1 tablespoon (15 mL) of your favourite hot sauce

A sprinkle or two of salt and lots of freshly ground pepper

FOR THE TACOS

8 crisp (not soft) corn taco shells

1 cup (250 mL) or so of grated Cheddar cheese

8 small soft flour tortillas

1/2 cup (125 mL) of sour cream

1/2 cup (125 mL) or so of your favourite salsa

1 cup (250 mL) or so of shredded lettuce

A handful of fresh tender cilantro sprigs

Preheat your oven to 450°F (230°C).

Splash the oil into your favourite heavy sauté pan or frying pan and heat it over medium-high heat. Add the ground beef, stirring to break it into smaller pieces. When the meat is cooked through but not browning, add the onion, garlic, chili powder, cumin, and oregano. Continue cooking and stirring until the onion softens and the spices smell great, 3 or 4 minutes. Add the tomatoes, ketchup, and hot sauce and simmer until everything is heated through, 2 or 3 minutes longer. Season to your taste with salt and pepper.

Divide the beef filling evenly among the corn taco shells. Top with a sprinkling of the cheese. Bake until the taco shells crisp and the cheese melts, about 2 minutes. Remove from the oven, then carefully wrap each crisp taco in a soft flour taco. Top with a dollop of sour cream, a spoonful of your favourite salsa, some shredded lettuce, and a sprig or two of cilantro. Serve and share!

KITCHEN TIP

This is a speedy taco filling. Because the meat is not browned, it doesn't toughen and thus it doesn't need a prolonged simmer to soften. The browned flavour is not missed among all the spicy southwestern flavours and aromas.

HOT AND COLD OLYMPIC CLUB SANDWICH

I led the team of Canadian chefs that cooked for the athletes of the world in the Whistler Athletes' Village during the 2010 Winter Olympic Games. We also served all the volunteers and staff in the village, and this sandwich was one of their favourites. It's addictively tasty and features a hot baked base mated with a cool crisp top. We made thousands, and every single one tasted amazing! **Serves 4**

FOR THE HOT BASE

4 boneless skinless chicken breasts

Olive oil for brushing

A pinch or two of salt and lots of freshly ground pepper

8 slices of bacon

4 ciabatta rolls, sliced in half lengthwise

1 cup (250 mL) of grated Cheddar cheese

FOR THE COLD TOP

2 tablespoons (30 mL) of mayonnaise

2 tablespoons (30 mL) of green hot dog relish

1 tablespoon (15 mL) of Dijon mustard

4 large leaves of leaf lettuce

1 large tomato, thinly sliced

1 red onion, thinly sliced

16 dill pickle slices

Begin with the hot base. Prepare and preheat your grill to its highest setting. Preheat your oven to 400°F (200°C).

Lightly flatten the chicken breasts with your hands or between two plates. Lightly oil each breast and season to your taste with salt and pepper. Grill, turning once or twice, until golden brown, about 10 minutes per side.

Place the bacon on a baking sheet and bake until crispy, about 10 minutes. Drain the bacon on a folded paper towel.

Arrange the chicken and bacon on the bottom of each roll. Top with a handful of the Cheddar cheese. Bake until the cheese melts and begins to brown, 5 to 10 minutes.

Meanwhile, make the cold top. Whisk together the mayonnaise, hot dog relish, and mustard. Spread the mixture evenly on the cut side of each sandwich top. Layer on the lettuce, tomato, onion, and dill pickle. Mate a crisp cold top roll to a freshly baked hot bottom roll. Serve and share!

KITCHEN TIP

Flattening the chicken breasts a bit before grilling helps in several ways. The meat cooks more evenly, it fits on the sandwich better, and it tastes better because there's more surface area for the grill to flavour and brown.

SALADS

Fennel Orange Beet Salad with Dill Dressing, 51

Bacon Lentil Salad with Arugula and Tarragon Mustard Dressing, 52

Baby Spinach and Bacon with Spicy Pickled Red Onions and Feta, 55

Buffalo "Wing" Salad with Spicy Chicken Chunks and Spicy Blue Cheese Dressing, 57

Pineapple Scallop Ceviche with Red Bell Pepper, Ginger, and Cilantro, 59

Iron Chef Battle Snack: Avocado, Tuna, and Tomatoes, 60

Asian Steak Salad with Spicy Peanut Slaw, 65

Italian Basil Salad with Crispy Parmesan and Oregano Vinaigrette, 66

Asian Salmon Salad with Miso Sesame Dressing, Edamame Beans, and Sprouts, 69

Southwestern Grilled Chicken Salad with Chipotle Lime Dressing and Tortilla Slivers, 70

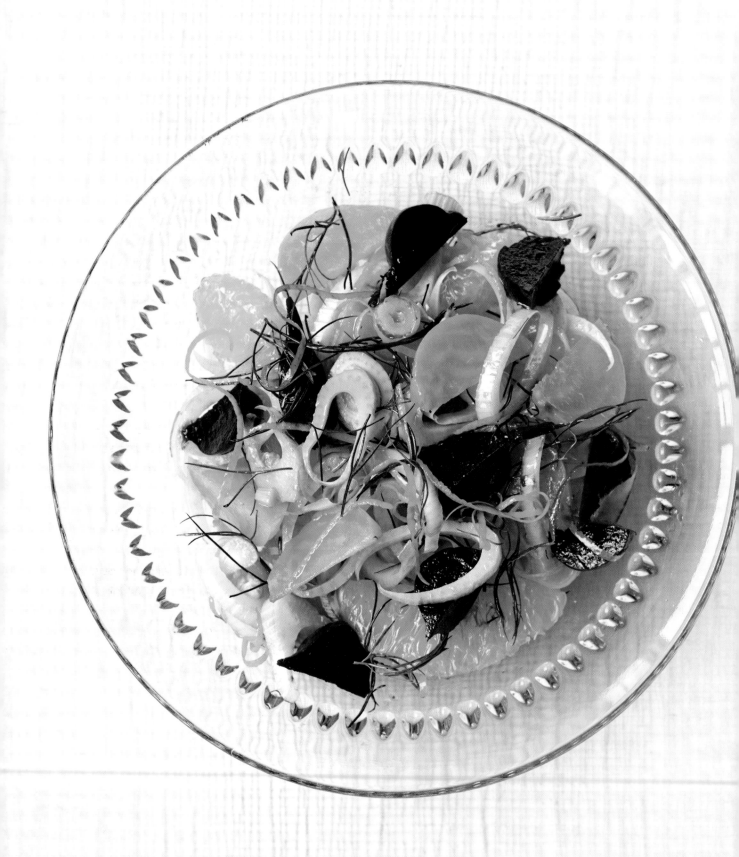

FENNEL ORANGE BEET SALAD
WITH DILL DRESSING

Beets are naturally very sweet, which may be why they're so tasty in this colourful salad. Roasting the beets produces a depth of earthy flavour that is perfectly accented by the tangy dill dressing and crisp licorice flavour and aroma of the fennel. **Makes 4 large salads or 8 smaller ones**

4 large beets, unpeeled, tops and bottoms trimmed off
1 fennel bulb
4 oranges
2 tablespoons (30 mL) of red wine vinegar
2 tablespoons (30 mL) of extra virgin olive oil
1 tablespoon (15 mL) of honey
1 tablespoon (15 mL) of Dijon mustard
1 cup (250 mL) or so of fresh dill sprigs, tougher stems discarded, finely chopped
A sprinkle or two of salt and lots of freshly ground pepper

Preheat your oven to 350°F (190°C).

Place the beets in a small ovenproof pot or baking dish along with 1/2 cup (125 mL) or so of water. Cover the pan with a tight-fitting lid or tightly seal it with foil. Roast until the beets are tender, 60 minutes or so depending on size. Uncover them, and when they're cool enough to handle, peel them—you'll find their skin slips off easily. Cut each beet into 8 wedges.

Meanwhile, cut the stalks from the fennel. Cut the bulb in half through the base, then cut out the tough, woody core at the base. Slice the remaining bulb crosswise as thinly as possible. Zest the oranges, then cut away the peel and pith and cut each orange into 8 wedges, discarding any seeds.

In a festive salad bowl, whisk together the orange zest, vinegar, olive oil, honey, and mustard. Add the beets, sliced fennel, orange wedges, and dill. Season to your taste with salt and pepper. Toss everything together until coated well with the dressing. Serve and share!

KITCHEN TIP

This salad may be served immediately or prepared a day in advance. If you decide to prep ahead, leave out the fresh dill. When you're ready to serve, add the dill—preserving its fresh flavour—then toss everything together once again.

BACON LENTIL SALAD WITH ARUGULA AND TARRAGON MUSTARD DRESSING

I love the wonderful earthy flavour and rich heartiness of lentils, and they're a wonderful base for this rustic salad. It's full of flavour with crisp bacon, spicy arugula, and a bright mustard vinaigrette finished and finessed with sharp tarragon. The result is classic Old World French country cooking at its best—simple, rustic, and addictively flavourful. **Serves 4 to 6**

1 cup (250 mL) of green lentils
8 slices of bacon, diced
2 tablespoons (30 mL) of extra virgin olive oil
2 tablespoons (30 mL) of red wine vinegar
2 tablespoons (30 mL) of coarse mustard
1/2 cup (125 mL) of chopped fresh tarragon
A sprinkle or two of salt and lots of freshly ground pepper
4 ounces (125 g) or so of arugula—a handful for everyone

Cook the lentils in a pot of simmering lightly salted water until they're tender and tasty but not completely soft—they're at their best when they retain just a touch of firmness—about 20 minutes. Drain and cool.

Meanwhile, in your favourite heavy frying pan over medium-high heat, cook the bacon until it's crisp. Drain the bacon on a few sheets of folded paper towel.

In a rustic salad bowl, whisk together the olive oil, vinegar, mustard, and tarragon until they form a smooth vinaigrette. Add the cooked lentils and bacon bits and season to your taste with salt and pepper. Toss everything together until the vinaigrette evenly coats the lentils and bacon. Serve over the arugula and share!

KITCHEN TIP

Lentils are seeds and thus very nutritious, but they're also tough and need vigorous cooking. But does boiling damage their nutrients and flavour? Actually, in much the same way that pasta survives a furious boil, very little of a lentil's flavour and thus very little of its nutrition are lost when they're simmered until tender. They're not very nutritious if you don't eat them, so this ancient method of tenderizing works very well.

BABY SPINACH AND BACON WITH SPICY PICKLED RED ONIONS AND FETA

Dark green baby spinach is packed full of dense nutrition and crunchy flavour, and it regularly appears on my table as my favourite salad green. Every now and then, though, I subvert spinach's healthiness with a whack of bacon bits and briny feta cheese tossed into this big bright salad. But pickled red onions are the star of the show. They're addictive and so easy to keep on hand for guest appearances in many of your future salad endeavours. **Serves 4 to 6**

FOR THE PICKLED RED ONIONS

1 cup (250 mL) of sugar

1 cup (250 mL) of red wine vinegar

1 teaspoon (5 mL) of your favourite hot sauce

A sprinkle or two of salt and lots of freshly ground pepper

1 large red onion, sliced into thin rounds

FOR THE SALAD

8 slices of bacon, diced

2 tablespoons (30 mL) of red wine vinegar

1 tablespoon (15 mL) of brown sugar

1 tablespoon (15 mL) of extra virgin olive oil

1 teaspoon (5 mL) of any mustard

8 to 10 ounces (250 to 300 g) of baby spinach

8 ounces (250 g) of feta cheese chunks

Begin with the pickled red onions. Put the sugar, vinegar, hot sauce, salt, and pepper into a small pot and bring to a boil, stirring occasionally. Add the onion and heat just long enough to return the mixture to a simmer, 2 or 3 minutes. Cool to room temperature. For best results, rest the mixture overnight in your refrigerator.

When it's salad time, brown the bacon pieces in your favourite heavy frying pan over medium-high heat until they're crispy. Remove them from the pan with a slotted spoon and drain on a few pieces of folded paper towel. Discard all but 1 tablespoon (15 mL) of the rendered fat.

In a small bowl, whisk together the bacon fat, vinegar, sugar, olive oil, and mustard until smooth. Just before serving, toss the dressing with the spinach leaves and top with the feta, bacon, and pickled red onions. Serve and share!

KITCHEN TIP

- Pickled red onions are one of my kitchen staples. They'll keep for months in the fridge so there's always a jar ready to top a variety of salads—tuna, avocado, tomato, chickpea. They're particularly good with smoked salmon and oysters.
- The mustard acts as an emulsifier, helping the oil, fat, and vinegar combine into a smooth dressing.

BUFFALO "WING" SALAD WITH SPICY CHICKEN CHUNKS AND SPICY BLUE CHEESE DRESSING

Some flavour combinations are irresistible no matter how they end up on your plate. This salad has it all: familiar flavours with lots of bright spiciness and crisp textures, all balanced with a pungent dressing. For absolute authenticity, make sure you use Frank's RedHot Original Cayenne Pepper Sauce, and have lots of cold beer on hand! **Serves 4 to 6**

FOR THE CHICKEN AND SAUCE

- 4 large boneless skinless chicken breasts
- 1 cup (250 mL) of all-purpose flour
- 2 tablespoons (30 mL) of cornstarch
- 1/4 cup (60 mL) of vegetable oil
- 1/2 cup (125 mL) of Frank's RedHot Original Cayenne Pepper Sauce
- 2 tablespoons (30 mL) of melted butter
- 1 tablespoon (15 mL) of molasses

FOR THE SALAD

- 4 ounces (125 g) of your favourite blue cheese
- 1/2 cup (125 mL) of mayonnaise
- 1 tablespoon (15 mL) of white vinegar
- 1 tablespoon (15 mL) of honey
- 1 head of iceberg lettuce (about 1 pound/500 g), cut into chunks
- 1 pint (500 mL) of cherry tomatoes, halved
- 2 celery stalks, thinly sliced
- 2 carrots, peeled and grated
- 2 green onions, thinly sliced

Cut the chicken into bite-size chunks and pat them dry on paper towels. Whisk together the flour and cornstarch. Toss the chicken with the flour mixture until all the chunks are evenly coated. Heat your favourite large sauté pan or frying pan over medium-high heat. Pour in the vegetable oil, and when it's hot, add the chicken. Pan-fry the chicken, turning as needed, until each piece is golden brown and crispy on all sides, about 15 minutes.

Meanwhile, prepare the Buffalo wing sauce. In a small bowl, whisk together the hot sauce, melted butter, and molasses. When the chicken is done, transfer it to a storage container with a tight-fitting lid. Pour in the sauce, fit the lid on tightly, and shake vigorously until the chicken is evenly coated.

In a salad bowl, use a fork to mash the blue cheese with some of the mayonnaise until it crumbles into small pieces. Stir in the rest of the mayo, the vinegar, and the honey. Add the lettuce, tomatoes, celery, carrots, and green onions and toss everything together until thoroughly coated and combined. Top with the spicy chicken chunks and sprinkle with any extra wing sauce. Serve and share!

KITCHEN TIP

The key to this salad is to replicate at home the authentic fried chicken flavour you get from a restaurant-grade deep-fryer: golden brown and crispy. So adjust the heat in the pan as high as you dare, patiently sizzling and browning the chicken until you're rewarded with caramelized chicken chunks. This salad will taste like you're out on the town!

PINEAPPLE SCALLOP CEVICHE WITH RED BELL PEPPER, GINGER, AND CILANTRO

Ceviche is my favourite beach food. I've eaten it in fancy restaurants, but it originated on hot tropical beaches, and that's where I found the best I've ever had. On the playa in Mexico, at a small table under an umbrella, there were bins of ceviche freshly made with that day's fish, several variations on a basic theme: fresh fish "cooked" in highly acidic citrus juice, then tossed with garnishing fruit or vegetables. I tried them all. This combo was my favourite, and the notes I took that day form the base for this recipe.
Serves 4

1/2 cup (125 mL) of freshly squeezed lime juice
2 tablespoons (30 mL) of grated frozen ginger
1 tablespoon (15 mL) of minced jalapeño
1 tablespoon (15 mL) of olive oil
1/4 teaspoon (1 mL) of salt
1 cup (250 mL) of finely cubed ripe pineapple
12 ounces (375 g) of the largest scallops you can find
1 red bell pepper, seeded and minced
1 small red onion, thinly sliced
1 cup (250 mL) of chopped cilantro leaves

In a large bowl, whisk together the lime juice, ginger, jalapeño, oil, and salt until smooth. Stir in the pineapple.

Pull away and discard the tough little side muscle from each scallop. Cut each scallop crosswise into 2 or 3 thin slices and add to the pineapple mixture. Stir well until the scallops are evenly coated. Cover and refrigerate for an hour or so.

Shortly before serving, prepare the bell pepper, red onion, and cilantro leaves. Gently toss them together, then fold them into the scallop mixture until everything is evenly coated. Serve and share!

KITCHEN TIP
This dish demands the absolutely freshest fish. Look your fishmonger in the eye and tell him you're making ceviche. He'll understand.

IRON CHEF BATTLE SNACK: AVOCADO, TUNA, AND TOMATOES

When I was invited to Kitchen Stadium to compete on *Iron Chef America*, I had no idea my favourite snack food would be the secret ingredient. So naturally, when avocados were revealed and the battle began, I made my favourite snack, the same way I always make it at home but jazzed up with some creative flourishes. It's lightning fast and very flavourful, perfect when the clock is ticking and your judges are ready to taste! **Serves 2**

1 can (6-1/2 ounces/184 g) of your favourite tuna
2 avocados, halved, pitted, scooped, and chopped
The zest and juice of 1 lemon
A thinly sliced green onion
A splash of your very best olive oil
A handful of cherry tomatoes, halved
A handful of chopped fresh parsley
A pinch or two of salt and lots of freshly ground pepper

Toss the tuna—juices and all—into a bowl and flake apart with a fork. Add everything else and toss gently until combined. Taste and adjust seasoning as needed. Serve and share!

KITCHEN TIP

To prep an avocado, follow these steps. Lay the avocado on your cutting board. Carefully slice lengthwise through the skin to the avocado's pit. Rotate the avocado, slicing all the way around the pit. Grasp each half and rotate them in opposite directions until one side releases. Set the piece with the pit on your cutting board. Using your largest, sharpest knife, firmly rap the pit with the blade. Twist until the pit pops out. Carefully slide a large spoon between the shell and the flesh, from one end to the other, easing out the flesh in one large piece.

LOCAL FLAVOUR

Local food keeps us connected to our lives. Our relentless pace can separate us from the myriad moments of life that pass us by daily. Locally sourced food helps us slow down and absorb the rhythms of nature, the colours of the season, and the stories that flavour our world.

Local food connections make good economic and environmental sense, but they're also sustained by the addictive strength of personally knowing the people who produce your food. Our food tastes best when we taste its story. When our cooking becomes personal, it grounds us to our community and connects us to life.

ASIAN STEAK SALAD
WITH SPICY PEANUT SLAW

The flavours of Asia are now mainstream and familiar to the average Western palate. This salad combines a tangy Asian-inspired vegetable slaw with a crunchy peanut dressing and the rich beefiness of grilled steak. It will taste right at home at your next picnic. **Serves 4**

A 12-ounce (375 g) sirloin steak
1 tablespoon (15 mL) of vegetable oil
A sprinkle or two of salt and lots of freshly ground pepper
1 cup (250 mL) of bean sprouts
1 cup (250 mL) of grated carrots
1 cup (250 mL) of snow peas, cut into long thin strips
1 cup (250 mL) of tender cilantro sprigs
1 cup (250 mL) of roasted peanuts
1/2 red onion, thinly sliced

FOR THE DRESSING

1/2 cup (125 mL) of smooth peanut butter
The zest and juice of 4 limes
1/4 cup (60 mL) of honey
1/4 cup (60 mL) of soy sauce
1 teaspoon (5 mL) of your favourite hot sauce
1/2 teaspoon (2 mL) of toasted sesame oil

Prepare and preheat your grill to its highest setting.

Rub the steak all over with the vegetable oil and season with salt and pepper. Grill until medium-rare, 5 or 6 minutes per side. Rest on a plate for a few minutes while you prepare the rest of the salad.

In your favourite serving bowl, make the dressing: whisk together the peanut butter, lime zest, lime juice, honey, soy sauce, hot sauce, and sesame oil. Add the bean sprouts, carrots, snow peas, cilantro, peanuts, and onion. Slice the rested steak into thin strips and add to the bowl, then toss everything together until well combined. Serve and share!

KITCHEN TIP

Resting the steak before slicing it helps boost this salad's flavour. As the meat rests it literally relaxes from the stress of its high-heat cooking. Its internal juices cool down a bit and the flesh reabsorbs them. When sliced, the meat retains its moisture and thus its flavour, adding immeasurably to the salad.

ITALIAN BASIL SALAD WITH CRISPY PARMESAN AND OREGANO VINAIGRETTE

The best salads are the simplest salads. This is one of my favourites because it's packed with so many simple Italian flavours. You'll love the old-school lettuce and tomatoes, the oregano-scented vinaigrette, the aromatic bursts of flavour that whole basil and parsley leaves add to the mix, and the delightful crunchiness of authentic Parmesan cheese grated and crisped in the oven. **Serves 4**

4 ounces (125 g) of Parmigiano-Reggiano cheese, grated
6 ounces (175 g) of mixed baby greens
2 cups (500 mL) of halved cherry tomatoes
1 cup (250 mL) or more of whole fresh basil leaves
1 cup (250 mL) or more of fresh Italian parsley leaves and tender stems
2 green onions, thinly sliced
A sprinkle or two of salt and lots of freshly ground pepper

FOR THE DRESSING

2 tablespoons (30 mL) of extra virgin olive oil
1 tablespoon (15 mL) of red wine vinegar
1 tablespoon (15 mL) of Dijon mustard
1 tablespoon (15 mL) of honey
1 teaspoon (5 mL) of dried oregano

Preheat your oven to 350°F (190°C). Lightly oil a baking sheet, then evenly sprinkle on a thin layer of the Parmesan cheese, forming a circle 8 inches (20 cm) or so wide. Bake until golden brown and crispy, about 10 minutes. Set the baking sheet on a rack to cool. Break the cheese into large chunks. (You can crisp the cheese several days in advance and store in an airtight container at room temperature.)

Just before serving, in a festive salad bowl, whisk together the oil, vinegar, mustard, honey, and oregano until they form a smooth vinaigrette. Add the greens, tomatoes, basil leaves, parsley leaves, and green onions. Season to your taste with salt and pepper. Toss everything together and top with the crispy Parmesan. Serve and share!

KITCHEN TIP

Authentic Parmigiano-Reggiano cheese is loaded with deep nutty flavours that dusty old canned "parmesan" can't begin to match. It's drier than most cheeses, which helps it quickly crisp and brown into a crunchy treat.

SOUTHWESTERN GRILLED CHICKEN SALAD WITH CHIPOTLE LIME DRESSING AND TORTILLA SLIVERS

The spicy flavours of the Southwest will make this brightly flavoured salad a memorable addition to your kitchen repertoire. You'll love the familiar flavours, the smokiness of the chipotle dressing, the aromatic bursts of flavour from the whole cilantro leaves, and the contrasting crunchiness of the easily made tortilla crisps. **Serves 4 to 6**

2 large corn or flour tortillas
2 large boneless skinless chicken breasts
A splash of cooking oil
A sprinkle or two of salt and lots of freshly ground pepper
2 ears of corn, freshly husked
The zest and juice of 2 limes
1/4 cup (60 mL) of olive oil
1 teaspoon (5 mL) of finely chopped canned chipotle chilies in adobo sauce
1/2 teaspoon (2 mL) of ground cumin
2 avocados, halved, seeded, scooped, and chopped
2 green onions, thinly sliced
1 cup (250 mL) of tender cilantro sprigs

Preheat your oven to 400°F (200°C). Prepare and preheat your grill to its highest setting.

First, crisp the tortilla strips. Roll the tortillas into a firm log shape, then slice crosswise into thin, even strips. Spread them on a baking sheet and bake until crisp and golden, about 15 minutes.

Meanwhile, brush both sides of the chicken breasts with a splash of cooking oil and season to your taste with salt and pepper. Grill them until golden brown, cooked through but still juicy, about 6 minutes per side. Rest on a plate until they cool. Meanwhile, grill the ears of corn, turning occasionally, until they're heated through and lightly charred, about 10 minutes.

In a festive salad bowl, whisk together the lime zest, lime juice, olive oil, chipotle, and cumin until they form a smooth dressing. Cut the corn kernels off the cobs directly into the bowl. Add the avocados and green onions. Season to your taste with salt and pepper. Toss everything together until the dressing evenly coats the salad. Thinly slice the grilled chicken and arrange it over the salad along with the cilantro sprigs and tortilla crisps. Serve and share!

KITCHEN TIP

Chipotle peppers are dried and smoked jalapeño peppers. They're available either dried or more commonly canned in adobo sauce, which is traditionally made with tomatoes, garlic, vinegar, and spices. They're very spicy, but the aromatic side to their flavour profile keeps pace, so a little bit goes a long way.

ASIAN SALMON SALAD WITH MISO SESAME DRESSING, EDAMAME BEANS, AND SPROUTS

This salad has three distinct parts that harmoniously become one: salmon seared and flaked into a salad of beans and bean sprouts, all tossed with an aromatic Asian-inspired dressing. But my favourite part is the crunchy chow mein noodles on top. **Serves 4**

1 salmon fillet (8 ounces/250 g), skin removed

A sprinkle or two of salt and lots of freshly ground pepper

A splash of cooking oil

1 cup (250 mL) of shelled edamame beans, thawed if frozen

1 cup (250 mL) of bean sprouts

1 cup (250 mL) of thinly sliced snow peas

1 cup (250 mL) of grated carrots

1 cup (250 mL) of cilantro leaves

2 green onions, thinly sliced

1 cup (250 mL) of crispy crunchy chow mein noodles

FOR THE DRESSING

1/4 cup (60 mL) of vegetable oil

1 tablespoon (15 mL) of toasted sesame oil

2 tablespoons (30 mL) of grated frozen ginger

2 tablespoons (30 mL) of rice wine vinegar

1 tablespoon (15 mL) of miso paste

1 teaspoon (5 mL) of soy sauce

1 teaspoon (5 mL) of honey

Preheat your favourite heavy sauté pan or frying pan over medium-high heat. Dry the salmon fillet on a piece or two of paper towel—this will help it sear and develop a crispy crust. Season the fish on both sides with salt and pepper to taste.

Add a splash of cooking oil to the pan, enough to evenly coat the bottom with a thin film. In a few moments, when the oil just begins to smoke, carefully slide in the salmon fillet. Increase the heat to high and sear the first side until golden brown and crunchy, 4 to 5 minutes. Flip the fish and continue searing until the fish is cooked through, another 4 or 5 minutes or so.

Meanwhile, make the dressing. In a salad bowl, whisk together the vegetable oil, sesame oil, ginger, vinegar, miso, soy sauce, and honey until smooth.

When the salmon is seared, add it to the salad bowl and break it into large flakes with a fork. Add the edamame beans, sprouts, snow peas, carrots, cilantro, and green onions and toss until everything is evenly coated with the dressing. Top with the crunchy chow mein noodles. Serve and share!

KITCHEN TIP

The best way to keep the salmon from sticking to the pan is to preheat the pan. Fish sticks to cold metal but not to hot metal. The oil will help, but nothing beats a hot pan for a nonstick cooking surface.

SOUTHWESTERN GRILLED CHICKEN SALAD WITH CHIPOTLE LIME DRESSING AND TORTILLA SLIVERS

The spicy flavours of the Southwest will make this brightly flavoured salad a memorable addition to your kitchen repertoire. You'll love the familiar flavours, the smokiness of the chipotle dressing, the aromatic bursts of flavour from the whole cilantro leaves, and the contrasting crunchiness of the easily made tortilla crisps. **Serves 4 to 6**

2 large corn or flour tortillas
2 large boneless skinless chicken breasts
A splash of cooking oil
A sprinkle or two of salt and lots of freshly ground pepper
2 ears of corn, freshly husked
The zest and juice of 2 limes
1/4 cup (60 mL) of olive oil
1 teaspoon (5 mL) of finely chopped canned chipotle chilies in adobo sauce
1/2 teaspoon (2 mL) of ground cumin
2 avocados, halved, seeded, scooped, and chopped
2 green onions, thinly sliced
1 cup (250 mL) of tender cilantro sprigs

Preheat your oven to 400°F (200°C). Prepare and preheat your grill to its highest setting.

First, crisp the tortilla strips. Roll the tortillas into a firm log shape, then slice crosswise into thin, even strips. Spread them on a baking sheet and bake until crisp and golden, about 15 minutes.

Meanwhile, brush both sides of the chicken breasts with a splash of cooking oil and season to your taste with salt and pepper. Grill them until golden brown, cooked through but still juicy, about 6 minutes per side. Rest on a plate until they cool. Meanwhile, grill the ears of corn, turning occasionally, until they're heated through and lightly charred, about 10 minutes.

In a festive salad bowl, whisk together the lime zest, lime juice, olive oil, chipotle, and cumin until they form a smooth dressing. Cut the corn kernels off the cobs directly into the bowl. Add the avocados and green onions. Season to your taste with salt and pepper. Toss everything together until the dressing evenly coats the salad. Thinly slice the grilled chicken and arrange it over the salad along with the cilantro sprigs and tortilla crisps. Serve and share!

KITCHEN TIP
Chipotle peppers are dried and smoked jalapeño peppers. They're available either dried or more commonly canned in adobo sauce, which is traditionally made with tomatoes, garlic, vinegar, and spices. They're very spicy, but the aromatic side to their flavour profile keeps pace, so a little bit goes a long way.

SOUPS

Coconut Mussel Broth with Ginger, Lime, and Cilantro, 75

Extra-Green Soup with Spinach, Broccoli, Peas, Parsley, and Green Onions, 76

Crab Corn Chowder with Bacon and Thyme, 79

Leftover Roast Chicken Broth with a Few Extra Things Thrown In, 80

Lentil Stew with Forty Garlic Cloves, 85

Manhattan Clam Chowder, 86

Split Pea Soup with Smoked Ham Hock, 90

Sweet Potato Vegetarian Chili with Cinnamon Sour Cream, 93

Sweet Potato Peanut Butter Soup with Moroccan Spice Roasted Peanuts, 94

Vegetarian Power Protein Soup with Two Grains and Two Legumes, 97

COCONUT MUSSEL BROTH WITH GINGER, LIME, AND CILANTRO

Mussels are perhaps the easiest fish of all to cook with. Their sweet briny flavour marries well with many flavour themes, including the Asian tastes of this recipe. Best of all, as mussels cook they release an incredibly rich broth that forms the base for this brightly flavoured soup. **Serves 4 to 6**

5 pounds (2.2 kg) or so of mussels, rinsed well
1 can (12 ounces/340 mL) of coconut milk
1 onion, thinly sliced
The zest and juice of 2 limes
2 tablespoons (30 mL) of grated frozen ginger
1 teaspoon (5 mL) of soy sauce
1 cup (250 mL) of tender cilantro sprigs
2 green onions, thinly sliced

Add the coconut milk, onion, lime zest, lime juice, ginger, and soy sauce to a large pot with a tight-fitting lid. Bring to a boil over medium-high heat. Reduce the heat to a simmer and simmer until the flavours of the aromatics thoroughly infuse the coconut milk, about 5 minutes.

Rinse the mussels well with lots of cool water, then toss them into the pot. Steam the mussels over medium-high heat until they cook through and their shells open, about 10 minutes. Discard any that haven't opened. Ladle into serving bowls, evenly dividing the mussels and their broth. Sprinkle on the green onions and cilantro. Serve and share!

KITCHEN TIP

- The vast majority of mussels available at your supermarket or fishmonger are cultivated, and most have had their beards removed. These tough threads help the mussel cling to underwater surfaces; if they're still present, just gently tug them off.

- Before you buy mussels, give them a good deep sniff—they should smell fresh and clean without any "fishy" aroma.

- You don't need to add any water to the pot when you steam mussels. They quickly release their own broth and happily steam away.

EXTRA-GREEN SOUP WITH SPINACH, BROCCOLI, PEAS, PARSLEY, AND GREEN ONIONS

Sometimes nutrition gets a bad rap in the flavour department, but this soup proves that healthful also means flavourful. It shows off the incredible nutritional density of dark green vegetables while revealing the aromatic flavours of these vital foods. It's as fun to eat as it is to look at! **Serves 4**

2 tablespoons (30 mL) of olive oil
4 garlic cloves, thinly sliced
1 large onion, diced
4 green onions, green and white parts sliced separately
3 cups (750 mL) of chicken broth, vegetable broth, or water
1 cup (250 mL) of whipping cream
1 bunch of broccoli, cut into small florets, tough stem peeled and thinly sliced
1 cup (250 mL) of fresh or frozen peas
1 tablespoon (15 mL) of fresh thyme leaves, or 1 teaspoon (5 mL) dried
6 ounces (175 g) of baby spinach
1 bunch of parsley, tougher stems discarded
A sprinkle or two of salt and lots of freshly ground pepper

Splash the olive oil into your favourite soup pot and heat it over medium-high heat. Toss in the garlic, onions, and the white part of the green onions. Sauté until the onions are tender but not brown, about 5 minutes. Pour in the broth and cream and bring to a simmer. Add the broccoli, peas, and thyme and simmer just until the broccoli is tender but still bright green, another 4 or 5 minutes. This will give the hardier vegetables a chance to cook before you add the more delicate ones.

Stir in the baby spinach, parsley, and green onion tops. Cook for just another minute or so until the spinach wilts and turns bright green. Season to your taste with salt and pepper.

At this point you may serve the soup as is, but if you have finicky eaters who don't like to see their green vegetables whole, purée the soup in a blender or food processor or with an immersion blender. For the smoothest results, strain the soup through your finest strainer. Serve and share!

KITCHEN TIP

Green vegetables are some of the healthiest possible foods you can eat, and the darker the green, the better. They're low in calories and fat, high in fibre, and packed with a laundry list of nutrients such as folic acid, vitamin C, potassium, magnesium, and various antioxidants and phytochemicals. A diet rich in green veggies has been proven to reduce the risk of many different cancers, improve vision, and strengthen your bones. Bottom line? Extra-green soup for all!

CRAB CORN CHOWDER WITH BACON AND THYME

This thick, rustic chowder is the first dish I make every year when our local corn comes into season. It's quite simply one of the very best ways to show off the sweetness of great corn—especially when you stir in lots of decadent crabmeat, crisp bacon, and aromatic fresh thyme! **Serves 4**

6 slices of bacon, sliced crosswise into narrow strips
1 large onion, finely chopped
2 celery stalks, diced
2 baking potatoes, diced
2 cups (500 mL) of fresh corn kernels
2 cups (500 mL) of chicken broth
2 cups (500 mL) of whipping cream
8 ounces (250 g) of fresh crabmeat, carefully picked over for any stray bits of shell
1/2 cup (125 mL) of chopped fresh parsley
1 tablespoon (15 mL) of chopped fresh thyme
A sprinkle or two of salt and lots of freshly ground pepper

Toss the bacon into your favourite soup pot over medium heat and cook it until lightly browned and crisp. Transfer to a few folded paper towels to drain. Pour off all but a tablespoon or two (15 to 30 mL) of the bacon fat. Add the onions and celery to the pot and cook, stirring frequently, until they're tender, about 5 minutes. Add the potatoes, corn, chicken broth, and cream and bring to a simmer. Simmer, stirring occasionally, until the potatoes are tender, another 10 minutes or so.

Just before serving, stir in the crab, parsley, and thyme. Simmer just long enough to heat everything through, another few minutes. Season with salt and pepper to your taste. Ladle the chowder into bowls and top with the reserved bacon. Serve and share!

KITCHEN TIP
The easiest way to remove the kernels from an ear of corn is to stand it up straight in a large bowl. Hold the ear with one hand and, using a serrated knife, firmly slice off the kernels, allowing them to fall into the bowl, which will also contain any splatter.

LEFTOVER ROAST CHICKEN BROTH WITH A FEW EXTRA THINGS THROWN IN

The leftovers from a roast chicken dinner are another meal just waiting to happen and one of your best opportunities to try freestyling your own flavours. Simmer the picked-over remains into a richly flavourful broth, then simply toss in a few kitchen staples. The results will taste like you meant to make soup all along! **Serves 4**

FOR THE BROTH

The bones and scraps from a leftover roast chicken

12 cups (3 L) of water

2 bay leaves

1 onion, chopped

1 carrot, chopped

1 celery stalk, chopped

A sprinkle or two of salt and lots of freshly ground pepper

FINISHING RICE, GRAINS, OR BEANS—1/2 CUP (125 ML) OF ANY ONE OF THE FOLLOWING:

any rice; any cooked bean; any lentil; any grain

FINISHING VEGETABLES—2 OR 3 CUPS (500 OR 750 ML) OF ANY COMBINATION OF THE FOLLOWING:

frozen green peas; frozen corn; frozen edamame beans; broccoli florets; cauliflower florets; chopped tomatoes; grated carrots; chopped zucchini; chopped bell peppers; thinly sliced green onions; grated sweet potato

FINISHING AROMATIC HERBS—ANY ONE OF THE FOLLOWING:

1 heaping tablespoon (20 mL) of chopped fresh thyme, sage, rosemary, or oregano

1/2 cup (125 mL) of chopped fresh basil or pesto

1 heaping teaspoon (6 mL) of dried thyme, sage, rosemary, oregano, or basil

When you're done enjoying your chicken dinner (and while someone else is doing the dishes), toss the remains into your favourite soup pot. Cover with the water and add the bay leaves, onions, carrots, and celery. Bring to a boil, then reduce the heat so the liquid is barely simmering. Cover and continue simmering for at least 1 hour or for as long as 2 or 3 hours. Skim off any scum that rises to the surface. The hot water will coax out all the flavour locked in the chicken bones and scraps, creating a rich, aromatic broth. Strain the broth and discard the remains except for any large chunks of meat that are worth saving. Continue making the soup or refrigerate the broth and meat for a day or two.

When you're ready to create your own personalized soup, bring the broth back to a simmer. Toss in your choice of a finishing rice, grain, or bean and simmer until tender, 20 to 45 minutes or so, depending on your choice.

Stir in the finishing vegetables and any reserved meat scraps. Continue simmering until everything is tender, another 10 minutes or so. In the last few minutes of cooking, add your choice of aromatic herbs—adding them last preserves their bright finishing flavour. Season with salt and pepper to your taste. Serve and share!

KITCHEN TIP

This is not so much a recipe as an idea, so feel free to personalize your soup as much as you like. Any vegetable or flavour theme is fair game.

LEFTOVER ROAST CHICKEN BROTH
WITH A FEW THINGS THROWN IN

LENTIL STEW WITH FORTY GARLIC CLOVES

If you love garlic, this dish is for you. Earthy lentils simmered into a stew with bacon and tomatoes are perfect for anchoring this garlic extravaganza. The garlic is prepared in two different ways, revealing two different flavours: mellow roasted garlic and a last-second finish with pungent, sizzling sautéed garlic.
Serves 4

40 garlic cloves, 30 cut in half, 10 minced
1/4 cup (60 mL) of olive oil
8 slices of bacon, sliced crosswise into narrow strips
1 large onion, chopped
1 large carrot, diced
1 cup (250 mL) of green lentils
1 can (28 ounces/796 mL) of diced tomatoes
4 cups (1 L) of chicken broth or water
1 tablespoon (15 mL) of dried thyme
1 tablespoon (15 mL) of any vinegar
A sprinkle or two of salt and lots of freshly ground pepper

Preheat your oven to 350°F (190°C).

In a small baking dish, toss the halved garlic cloves with 2 tablespoons (30 mL) of the oil. Roast, stirring now and then, until the garlic is golden brown and soft, about 30 minutes.

Meanwhile, begin making the soup. In your favourite soup pot over medium-high heat, cook the bacon until lightly browned and crisp. Drain on a few folded paper towels. Pour off all but a tablespoon or two (15 to 30 mL) of the bacon fat. Add the onions and carrots to the pot and sauté, stirring frequently, until they're tender, about 5 minutes. Add the lentils, tomatoes, broth, and thyme and bring to a boil. Reduce the heat so the liquid is barely simmering and simmer, uncovered and stirring occasionally, until the lentils are tender, about 45 minutes. When the roasted garlic cloves are done, stir them in as well.

Shortly before serving, stir in the bacon and vinegar. Season to your taste with salt and pepper.

Splash the remaining 2 tablespoons (30 mL) oil into a sauté pan and heat it over medium-high heat. Add the minced garlic and sauté, stirring occasionally, until it sizzles and begins to lightly brown, 3 or 4 minutes. Immediately head for the table and theatrically pour the sizzling garlic oil over the stew. Serve and share!

KITCHEN TIP
Patiently roasting the garlic removes its pungency while producing a deep aromatic flavour. A splash of vinegar acts as a secret ingredient, adding brightness and mysteriously enhancing all the stew's flavours without announcing its sour presence.

MANHATTAN CLAM CHOWDER

This classic version of clam chowder is based on tomatoes, not dairy, so it's lighter and brighter than its heavier cream-based cousin. Like any great chowder, it's the perfect way to start a meal, although it's hearty enough to serve as the main course too. **Serves 4 to 6**

2 tablespoons (30 mL) of olive oil
1 large onion, finely chopped
4 garlic cloves, minced
2 celery stalks, diced
1 green bell pepper, seeded and diced
1 baking potato, peeled and diced
2 cans (each 5 ounces/142 g) of clams
1 can (28 ounces/796 mL) of chopped tomatoes
2 cups (500 mL) of tomato juice
1 teaspoon (5 mL) of dried thyme
A sprinkle or two of salt and lots of freshly ground pepper
1 cup (250 mL) of chopped fresh parsley (about 1 bunch)

Splash the olive oil into your favourite soup pot and heat it over medium-high heat. Sauté the onions, garlic, celery, and bell pepper until they're bright and tender but not browned, about 10 minutes. Add the potato, clams and their liquid, tomatoes, tomato juice, and thyme and bring everything to a boil. Reduce the heat so the liquid is just barely simmering and simmer, stirring occasionally, until the potatoes are tender, about 20 minutes.

Just before serving, season the soup to your taste with salt and pepper. Stir in the parsley at the last second to preserve its fresh aromatic flavour. Serve and share!

KITCHEN TIP

Fresh parsley is often overlooked as a herb and tends to be thought of as just a pretty garnish. In fact it's packed with aromatic flavours that brighten this soup and many other dishes. Because its flavours are delicate, parsley is best when it's added last—too much heat will damage and diminish its brightness.

MEDIUM-HIGH HEAT

In today's kitchen it's easy to apply a lot of heat to your food in a hurry. Controlling the heat is easy at the extremes—full-on boil or bare simmer. But what about the sweet spot in the middle, the browning zone? That takes real skill. Too hot and you burn your food, too low and no flavour develops.

The key is vigilance and observation. In essence, be present. Be prepared to make small adjustments until you instinctively find the harmonious place where your gear and ingredients mesh. There's no substitute for experience!

SPLIT PEA SOUP WITH SMOKED HAM HOCK

This hearty soup is packed full of rich smoky ham and two different pea flavours. Dried peas give it traditional earthiness, while a last-minute addition of green peas brightens the flavour. This is my favourite soup for a cold winter day. **Serves 6 to 8**

2 tablespoons (30 mL) of any vegetable oil
1 large onion, chopped
1 large carrot, chopped
1 cup (250 mL) of dried split green peas
1 smoked ham hock
8 cups (2 L) of chicken broth or water
1 teaspoon (5 mL) of dried thyme
2 bay leaves
1 cup (250 mL) of frozen or freshly shucked green peas
2 heaping tablespoons (40 mL) of Dijon mustard
A sprinkle or two of salt and lots of freshly ground pepper

Splash the oil into your favourite soup pot and heat it over medium-high heat. Toss in the onions and carrots and sauté until they're tender, about 10 minutes. Add the split peas, ham hock, water, thyme, and bay leaves. Bring to a boil, then reduce the heat so the liquid is barely simmering. Simmer, covered and stirring occasionally, until the peas and ham hock are tender, about 1 hour. If you like, you may simmer the soup in a slow cooker for several hours or longer.

Shortly before serving, remove the ham hock. Trim away and discard the skin and fat. Pull and shred the meat into smaller pieces, then toss them back into the soup. Add the green peas and simmer just long enough to heat them through, another few minutes. Stir in the mustard. Season to your taste with salt and pepper. Serve and share!

KITCHEN TIP

- Ham hocks are the ankle of the pig, so they're very tough, but they're also packed with flavour. Because they're tough, they are also inexpensive, so they're ideal for flavouring soup.

- You can discard the bay leaves before serving or leave them in like I do. Whoever gets one in their bowl has to help wash the dishes!

SWEET POTATO VEGETARIAN CHILI WITH CINNAMON SOUR CREAM

Few things are as comforting as a warm, steaming bowl of chili. This vegetarian version is packed with so much flavour you won't notice the missing meat. You will notice the familiar rustic flavours, the earthy sweetness of the sweet potatoes, and the colourful nutrition they bring to your table. **Serves 4 to 6**

2 tablespoons (30 mL) of vegetable oil

1 large onion, chopped

1 green bell pepper, seeded and chopped

8 garlic cloves, thinly sliced

1 tablespoon (15 mL) of cumin seeds

1 tablespoon (15 mL) of chili powder

1 tablespoon (15 mL) of dried oregano

2 cups (500 mL) of fresh or frozen corn

1 can (14 ounces/398 mL) of black beans, rinsed and drained

1 can (14 ounces/398 mL) of kidney beans, rinsed and drained

1 can (28 ounces/796 mL) of whole tomatoes

1 sweet potato, peeled and finely diced

1 tablespoon (15 mL) of chopped canned chipotle chilies in adobo sauce

1/2 cup (125 mL) of sour cream

1 teaspoon (5 mL) of cinnamon

A sprinkle or two of salt

1 cup (250 mL) of tender cilantro sprigs

2 green onions, thinly sliced

Heat the oil in your favourite soup pot over medium-high heat. Toss in the onions and green pepper and sauté, stirring frequently, until the vegetables begin to brown, 6 or 8 minutes. Stir in the garlic, cumin seeds, chili powder, and oregano. Reduce the heat to medium and cook, stirring, until the spices are very fragrant, another 2 minutes or so.

Stir in the corn, black beans, and kidney beans. Add the juice from the canned tomatoes, then coarsely chop the tomatoes and add them as well. Add the sweet potatoes and chipotle chilies. Bring to a boil, then reduce the heat so the liquid is just barely simmering. Simmer, stirring frequently, until the sweet potatoes are tender and the chili begins to thicken, 20 to 25 minutes.

Meanwhile, stir together the sour cream and cinnamon. Just before serving, season the chili to your taste with salt. Ladle into serving bowls and top with the sour cream and a tangle of cilantro and green onions. Serve and share!

KITCHEN TIP

Most of us easily meet our protein needs by eating meat. Vegetarians do so by enjoying grains and legumes. Both grains and legumes contain essential protein building blocks, but neither contains all of them. Together, though, they complement each other (like the corn and beans in this soup), providing all the life-giving protein nutrients a vegetarian needs.

SWEET POTATO PEANUT BUTTER SOUP WITH MOROCCAN SPICE ROASTED PEANUTS

Few cuisines are as flavourful as Morocco's, one of my favourite places to visit. The many colourful and aromatic spices I found in the ancient souks of Marrakesh inspire this soup. At first glance these flavours may seem odd together, but one taste will convince you otherwise. The spices beautifully complement the sweet earthiness of the sweet potatoes and the rich creaminess of the peanut butter. The results are addictively flavourful. **Serves 4 to 6**

FOR THE PEANUTS

1 teaspoon (5 mL) of chili powder
1/2 teaspoon (2 mL) of cinnamon
1/2 teaspoon (2 mL) of ground cumin
1/2 teaspoon (2 mL) of ground coriander
1/2 teaspoon (2 mL) of nutmeg
1 tablespoon (15 mL) of honey
1 tablespoon (15 mL) of butter
1 cup (250 mL) of raw peanuts
1 tablespoon (15 mL) of sugar

FOR THE SOUP

2 tablespoons (30 mL) of olive oil
1 large onion, diced
4 garlic cloves, thinly sliced
6 cups (1.5 L) of chicken broth or water
1 sweet potato, peeled and grated
1/2 cup (125 mL) of peanut butter
A sprinkle or two of salt and lots of freshly
  ground pepper

Preheat your oven to 350°F (190°C).

Whisk together the spices and reserve 1 teaspoon (5 mL) for the peanuts. Set aside the rest for the soup. In a small pot, bring the honey and butter to a bubbling simmer over medium-high heat. Stir in the peanuts until they're evenly coated. Spread in a single layer on a baking sheet and roast, stirring occasionally, until golden brown and fragrant, 15 to 20 minutes. Scrape the peanuts into a bowl and toss with the sugar and the reserved teaspoon of spice.

Meanwhile, begin the soup. Splash the oil into your favourite soup pot and heat it over medium-high heat. Add the onions, garlic, and reserved spices and sauté until the onion is tender and golden brown, about 10 minutes. Pour in the broth and toss in the sweet potato and peanut butter. Bring to a boil, then reduce the heat so the liquid is barely simmering. Simmer, stirring occasionally, until the sweet potatoes are tender, 15 minutes or so.

Purée the soup in a blender or food processor or with your immersion blender. For the smoothest results, strain the soup through your finest strainer. Reheat the soup before serving. Season it to your taste with salt and pepper. Ladle it into soup bowls and top with a sprinkling of the peanuts. Serve and share!

KITCHEN TIP

The ground spices in your kitchen were likely ground a long time ago in a factory far, far away and then endured a long trip to your shelves. As a result, their flavours may have become tired and dull. Toasting them in the hot oil with the onions brightens their flavours, dramatically adding much to the soup.

VEGETARIAN POWER PROTEIN SOUP WITH TWO GRAINS AND TWO LEGUMES

Meat eaters get vital protein from our top-of-the-food-chain meat-based diets, while vegetarians rely on a daily blend of grains and legumes. This soup features two of each: on the grain side brown rice and corn, and on the legume side lentils and peas. Together they add up to lots of powerful nutrition that proves healthy tastes great! **Serves 6 to 8**

2 tablespoons (30 mL) of any vegetable oil
1 large onion, finely diced
4 garlic cloves, minced
1 large carrot, shredded
1 cup (250 mL) or so of chopped button mushrooms
1/2 cup (125 mL) of brown rice
1/2 cup (125 mL) of green lentils
8 cups (2 L) of water
2 bay leaves
1 tablespoon (15 mL) of chopped fresh thyme
1 cup (250 mL) of fresh or frozen corn
1 cup (250 mL) of fresh or frozen peas
A sprinkle or two of salt and lots of freshly ground pepper

Splash the oil into your favourite soup pot and heat it over medium-high heat. Toss in the onions, garlic, carrot, and mushrooms. Sauté until the vegetables are tender and just starting to brown, about 15 minutes.

Add the brown rice, lentils, water, bay leaves, and thyme. Bring everything to a boil, then reduce the heat so the liquid is barely simmering. Simmer, uncovered and stirring occasionally, until the rice and lentils are tender, about 40 minutes.

Just before serving, stir in the corn and peas. Continue heating just long enough to heat them through. Discard the bay leaves. Season the soup to your taste with salt and pepper. Serve and share!

KITCHEN TIP

You may replace the brown rice with any grain without compromising the flavour or nutritional content of this soup. Barley, wheat berries, oats, and any rice all work well. The same is true for the lentils. You can use any dried beans or even chickpeas, but to speed up the cooking time, soak them overnight in water first, then rinse and drain them before adding to the soup.

FISH

LOCAL OYSTERS WITH BLOODY MARY ICE

Shuck a bucket of oysters with friends for a fun get-together. Top them with a scoop of Bloody Mary ice and you'll have an instant party! **Makes enough for a party**

1 can (14 ounces/398 mL) of diced tomatoes
1/2 cup (125 mL) of vodka or aquavit
1/2 cup (125 mL) of sugar
1 teaspoon (5 mL) of Worcestershire sauce
1 teaspoon (5 mL) of your favourite hot sauce
1/2 cup (125 mL) or so of freshly squeezed lemon juice
1/4 teaspoon (1 mL) of salt
4 dozen fresh oysters

In your blender or food processor, purée the tomatoes, vodka, sugar, Worcestershire sauce, hot sauce, lemon juice, and salt. Pour into a shallow dish and place in your freezer. Every 30 minutes or so, stir and scrape the mixture with a fork until it's frozen and granular. It's best to make the ice the day before you'd like to serve it; cover with plastic wrap and keep frozen.

When your friends arrive, shuck away. Top each oyster with a spoonful of the Bloody Mary ice.
Serve and share!

KITCHEN TIP
This ice takes advantage of alcohol and sugar's inability to freeze. Working together, the two ingredients keep the ice from becoming rock solid. Stirring the mixture as it begins to freeze also helps keep it soft.

SPEEDY SHRIMP PENNE WITH CHARDONNAY CREAM CHEESE SAUCE

Pasta and shrimp are made for each other. So are this dish's two secret ingredients: shrimp shells, packed with lots of easily released bonus shrimp flavour, and cream cheese, which melts into an instant tangy, creamy sauce. This is a pasta sauce you can make in the time it takes the penne to cook. **Serves 4**

1 pound (500 g) of shrimp, shells reserved, each shrimp cut into 4 chunks
1 carrot, grated
1 bay leaf
2 cups (500 mL) of chardonnay
1 pound (500 g) of penne
1 cup (250 mL) or so of softened cream cheese
2 tablespoons (30 mL) of Dijon mustard
1/2 cup (125 mL) of chopped fresh tarragon
2 green onions, thinly sliced
A sprinkle or two of salt and lots of freshly ground pepper

Put the shrimp shells, carrot, bay leaf, and wine in a small saucepan and bring to a boil over medium-high heat. Reduce the heat so the liquid is barely simmering. Cover and simmer for 10 minutes or so.

Meanwhile, bring a large pot of salted water to a boil. Cook the penne until it's nearly tender but not quite done. Add the shrimp to the boiling water and cook until the shrimp is cooked through and the pasta is tender, another 2 minutes or so.

Drain the pasta and shrimp and return them to the pot. Toss in the cream cheese and mustard. Strain in the wine mixture, pressing every last drop of nectar out of the shrimp shells. Toss in a few spoonfuls of the carrots minus the shells. Stir everything together until the cream cheese melts and forms a smooth, creamy sauce. Stir in the tarragon and green onions. Lightly season to your taste with salt and pepper.
Serve and share!

KITCHEN TIP
Normally, shrimp shells are thrown out, but there's actually more shrimp flavour in the shell than in the shrimp itself. Fortunately, that flavour is very easy to release—a short simmer in any liquid will quickly create an aromatic broth.

GRILLED TUNA STEAK WITH WHITE BEAN ARUGULA SALAD AND ANCHOVY DRESSING

Grilling tuna is one of my favourite ways to enjoy this filet mignon of the sea. Tuna's rich fattiness and luxurious texture allow it to grill as easily as any meat, and it's at its best when its centre stays cool. Tuna's big grill flavours work well with other strong flavours, like briny anchovy dressing over a rich white bean salad tossed with sharp, peppery arugula. **Serves 4**

1 cup (250 mL) of dried white beans, soaked overnight in 2 cups (500 mL) of water, or
  1 can (14 ounces/398 mL) of white beans, rinsed and drained
8 oil-packed anchovies, drained and patted dry
The zest and juice of 1 lemon
2 tablespoons (30 mL) of olive oil
1 tablespoon (15 mL) of grainy mustard
2 handfuls of arugula leaves (about 4 ounces/125 g)
2 green onions, thinly sliced
A sprinkle or two of salt and lots of freshly ground pepper
4 fresh tuna steaks (each 8 ounces/250 g and at least 1 inch/2.5 cm thick), patted dry
1/4 cup (60 mL) of olive oil

If you're using dried beans, simmer them until tender, about an hour and possibly longer. Drain and set aside while you ready the salad. In a salad bowl, mash the anchovies into a thick paste with a fork. Add the lemon zest, lemon juice, oil, and mustard, then continue mashing until you form a smooth dressing. Season to your taste with salt and pepper. Add the beans and toss until they're thoroughly coated with the dressing. Top with the arugula and green onions but—for maximum crispiness—wait until just before serving to toss them with the marinating beans.

Prepare and preheat your grill to its highest setting.

Rub the tuna steaks with the olive oil. Lightly season the fish to your taste with salt and pepper. Grill, turning once, until the fish is cooked to your liking, 3 to 5 minutes per side for rare, 5 to 7 minutes for medium. Finish tossing the salad, then portion onto 4 plates and top with a slab of grilled tuna. Serve and share!

KITCHEN TIP

Several types of fresh tuna are typically available from your fishmonger. The most common choice is bigeye or ahi, which is prized for its bright red flesh and rich flavour. Yellowfin is paler and also commonly available. Bluefin, the richest and meatiest of all, is rarely seen in markets, as most ends up in the hands of high-end sushi chefs or on a fast ride to the fish markets of Japan.

PAN-SEARED SCALLOPS WITH HOUSE WINE SAUCE

Searing sweet briny scallops to give them a golden brown crispy crust is an essential cooking method for any cook's seafood repertoire. The secret is a hot pan, a high-heat, rapid cooking trick mastered by busy restaurant line cooks. A hot pan not only browns the scallops but allows you to whip up a tasty wine sauce too. **Serves 4**

1 pound (500 g) or more of large fresh sea scallops, small tough side muscle removed, patted dry
1 cup (250 mL) of all-purpose flour
A sprinkle or two of salt and lots of freshly ground pepper
1 tablespoon (15 mL) of any cooking oil
2 tablespoons (30 mL) of butter
4 garlic cloves, thinly sliced
2 green onions, white and green parts thinly sliced separately
1 cup (250 mL) of your favourite dry wine
1 teaspoon (5 mL) of Dijon mustard
1/2 cup (125 mL) of whipping cream

Preheat your largest, heaviest frying pan over medium-high heat for a few minutes. Meanwhile, toss the scallops in the flour and season them to your taste with salt and pepper. Splash the oil into the hot pan, gently swirling until the oil is shimmering hot but not smoking. Add the butter to the side of the pan where the oil gathers and pools. When the butter has melted, swirl the pan for a moment or two until the butter just begins to brown and sizzle. When the butter is golden brown and fragrant, quickly add the scallops one at a time, in a single layer with a bit of space in between. Watch and listen to the still-browning butter. Adjust the heat so it's high enough to maintain a sizzling sear but not so high that the butter begins to burn. Continue searing the scallops, turning them once, until they're evenly browned on both sides, 5 to 7 minutes. Transfer the caramelized scallops to a platter and cover loosely with foil to keep warm.

Toss the garlic and the white part of the green onions into the pan and sauté them briefly until they're soft and aromatic, 2 minutes or so. Pour in the wine and simmer until half of it has evaporated. Whisk in the mustard, then stir in the cream and reduce until the sauce smoothes and thickens, another minute or two. Remove from the heat and stir in the green onion tops. Pour the sauce over the scallops. Serve and share!

KITCHEN TIP

As the wine reduces, the sauce will thicken, but without mustard, the wine and butter mixture will be unstable and eventually separate. Mustard contains lecithin, an emulsifier, which stabilizes the sauce by encouraging the oil and water to combine smoothly.

TORTILLA-CRUSTED WHITEFISH WITH SALSA SALSA

This multicoloured dish is a great way to get kids to eat fish. Crisp tortilla chips are perfect for crusting—they're full of built-in crunch and familiar tasty texture. Your favourite zesty salsa jazzed up with a few fresh ingredients will help too. Together, all these familiar flavours just might persuade your finicky eater to try seafood! **Serves 4**

1 cup (250 mL) of all-purpose flour

2 eggs, lightly beaten

2 cups (500 mL) of hand-crumbled multicoloured tortilla chips

A sprinkle or two of salt and lots of freshly ground pepper

4 skinned fillets of any whitefish (about 1-1/2 pounds/750 g in total), patted dry

FOR THE SALSA

1/2 cup (125 mL) of your favourite salsa

1/2 cup (125 mL) of cherry tomatoes, halved

1/2 cup (125 mL) of cilantro leaves and tender stems

1/2 teaspoon (2 mL) of minced jalapeño

2 green onions, thinly sliced

The zest and juice of 1 lime

1 tablespoon (15 mL) of olive oil

Preheat your oven to 400°F (200°C). Lightly oil a baking sheet.

Put the flour, eggs, and tortilla chips into 3 separate bowls. Season the flour. Working with one fillet at a time, dredge the fillet in the flour, coating it evenly and shaking off any excess. Dip the fillet into the egg, coating it evenly and holding it up to drain for a few moments. Finally, dip the fillet into the tortilla chips, turning, pressing, and sprinkling as needed so the crust adheres. Place the fish on the baking sheet. Repeat with the remaining fillets. Bake until the fish is cooked through and crusty, 10 to 15 minutes. The fish is done when a meat thermometer inserted in the thickest part registers 130°F (55°C).

Meanwhile, toss together the salsa salsa. In a small bowl, mix the prepared salsa with the tomatoes, cilantro, jalapeño, green onions, lime zest and juice, and olive oil. Arrange the finished fish on a serving platter and top with the salsa. Serve and share!

KITCHEN TIP

Cherry tomatoes usually have more vine-ripened flavour than their larger green-picked cousins in your supermarket. That true aromatic flavour shines through in this simple improvised salsa that brightens and builds from your favourite salsa.

SMOKED SALMON-CRUSTED SALMON WITH CUCUMBER-DILL PICKLE

This distinctive dish features two salmons for the price of one—a simply baked fillet under a crunchy smoked salmon crust. It's an irresistible way to stretch a little bit of luxurious smoked salmon into a lot of flavour, and it makes a special dinner-party dish. **Serves 4**

1 cup (250 mL) of fresh or dry bread crumbs

1/4 cup (60 mL) of softened butter

4 ounces (125 g) of smoked salmon

4 centre-cut salmon fillets
(each about 6 ounces/175 g), patted dry

A sprinkle or two of salt and lots of
freshly ground pepper

FOR THE PICKLE

1 large cucumber, peeled and diced

1 dill pickle, diced

1 cup (250 mL) of chopped fresh dill sprigs,
thicker stems discarded

2 green onions, thinly sliced

1 tablespoon (15 mL) of cider vinegar

1 tablespoon (15 mL) of honey

A sprinkle or two of salt and lots of freshly
ground pepper

Preheat your oven to 400°F (200°C). Lightly oil a baking sheet.

Begin with the cucumber pickle. In a bowl, toss together the cucumber, dill pickle, dill, green onions, vinegar, and honey. Lightly season to your taste with salt and pepper, and put aside.

Put the bread crumbs and butter into your food processor and pulse until they form a crumbly paste. Add the smoked salmon and pulse just long enough to coarsely chop it, mixing it into the paste. Lightly season the salmon fillets with salt and pepper to your taste. With your hands, spread one-quarter of the paste in a thick, even layer across the top of each fillet. Place the salmon on the baking sheet and bake until crusty, 12 to 15 minutes.

Serve and share the salmon fillets with the pickle.

KITCHEN TIP

Conveniently, fish cooks much more quickly than meat, but that means it also dries out much faster too. To preserve its flavourful moisture, try not to overcook it. Salmon is actually at its best when the centre is still a bit pink, similar to medium-rare beef. If you're not sure whether it's done, simply make a small cut in the side and have a peek.

SERVING AND

Who's at the table is far more important than what's on the table.

As cooks, it's so easy to get caught up in the process, the simple joy

of cooking, that we lose sight of why we cook to begin with. We're at

our best when we share.

SHARING

Food is really just one part of a meal. As brilliant as your creations may be, full of artful flavours and impeccably sourced ingredients, they're not the main event. Spending time with your friends, family, and community is the real occasion. It's wonderful to be the cook, to facilitate our time together by simply sharing our best.

SLOW-BAKED SALMON WITH HONEY MUSTARD GLAZE

Since salmon is a fatty fish, it's often cooked quickly with high, searing heat that gives it a crispy crust. But salmon is just as delicious when it's cooked slowly. Gentle, patient heating gives it a tender, melt-in-your-mouth texture that is truly memorable—especially when it's brightened with a simple honey mustard glaze. **Serves 4**

2 tablespoons (30 mL) of honey
2 tablespoons (30 mL) of your favourite mustard
1 tablespoon (15 mL) of soy sauce
1 teaspoon (5 mL) of your favourite hot sauce
4 centre-cut salmon fillets (each about 6 ounces/175 g), skinned and patted dry

Preheat your oven to the low, low temperature of 225°F (110°C). Lightly oil a roasting pan.

Whisk together the honey, mustard, soy sauce, and hot sauce. Arrange the fillets in the roasting pan skin side down, leaving an inch or two of space in between each one. Spread the glaze evenly over the salmon.

Bake until the salmon is cooked through and opaque but still juicy, about 30 minutes. Serve and share!

KITCHEN TIP
The gentle heat of this cooking method gives the salmon an incredibly luscious texture that you may not have enjoyed before. It's a delicate way to show off the fish's natural flavours while revealing a smooth luxurious mouth feel.

SPICY ORANGE-POACHED SALMON WITH GINGER SOY MARMALADE

Poaching is one of the simplest ways to cook any fish. This time-tested method is as easy as simmering the fish in any flavourful liquid. Poaching highlights the delicate texture of salmon while simultaneously adding lots of aromatic flavour. **Serves 4**

2 tablespoons (30 mL) of olive oil

1 large onion, diced

8 garlic cloves, thinly sliced

4 cups (1 L) of orange juice

The zest and juice of 2 lemons

1 teaspoon (5 mL) of your favourite hot sauce

2 bay leaves

4 centre-cut salmon fillets
(each about 6 ounces/175 g), patted dry

A sprinkle or two of salt and lots of freshly
ground pepper

FOR THE MARMALADE

1/2 cup (125 mL) of orange marmalade

2 tablespoons (30 mL) of grated frozen ginger

1 tablespoon (15 mL) of soy sauce

2 green onions, thinly sliced

In a saucepan that's just big enough to hold the salmon fillets in a single layer, heat the oil over medium-high heat. Sauté the onions and garlic until they're golden brown, about 5 minutes. Add the orange juice, lemon zest, lemon juice, hot sauce, and bay leaves. Bring the poaching liquid to a full boil, then reduce the heat so the liquid is barely simmering. Slide in the salmon fillets and gently poach until they're barely cooked through, about 10 minutes.

Meanwhile, stir together the marmalade, ginger, soy sauce, and green onions. Gently place each salmon fillet in a shallow bowl. Top with a ladle of the simmering poaching broth and a dollop of the marmalade. Serve and share!

KITCHEN TIP

The poaching broth's job is to add more flavour to the fish than it takes away. If fish is poached in plain water, it will lose flavour while the water gains flavour. A good poaching liquid like this one is flavoured so strongly that the fish can't help but absorb lots of aromatic flavour. You may judge the salmon's doneness with a meat thermometer: when it reaches 130°F (55°C) it's done, or 140°F (60°C) if you prefer it a bit more well done.

GRILLED SALMON WITH GRILLED TOMATO, BASIL, AND CAPER SALAD

The high fat content of salmon makes it ideal for grilling. It easily absorbs the smoky, charred flavours of the grill and is wonderful served with just about any topping, sauce, or condiment. Tomatoes are great on the grill too, where they slowly roast, softening and intensifying in flavour. Chopped and tossed with aromatic basil and tangy capers, they form an ideal topping for the grilled salmon. **Serves 4**

4 centre-cut salmon fillets (each about 6 ounces/175 g), patted dry
2 tablespoons (30 mL) of olive oil
A sprinkle or two of salt and lots of freshly ground pepper
4 ripe plum tomatoes, halved
2 green onions
1 cup (250 mL) of fresh basil leaves
1 tablespoon (15 mL) of drained capers
1 tablespoon (15 mL) of red wine vinegar

Prepare and preheat your grill to its highest setting.

Lightly oil the salmon fillets, then lightly season them to your taste with salt and pepper. Place the fish diagonally across the grates. Grill, turning once or twice, until the fish is golden brown and cooked through, 10 to 12 minutes.

At the same time, lightly oil the tomatoes, then place them cut side down on the grill along with the green onions. Lightly char them, turning once or twice. Transfer the tomatoes to a small bowl and crush with a fork. Chop the green onions and toss in along with the whole basil leaves, the capers, and the vinegar. Lightly season to your taste with salt and pepper. Toss everything together and spoon over the grilled salmon. Serve and share!

KITCHEN TIP
Unlike most herbs, basil's flavour is light and bright enough that the leaves can be enjoyed whole like a salad green without having to be cut into smaller pieces.

MEDITERRANEAN BRAISED SALMON WITH RIPE TOMATOES, OLIVES, AND OREGANO

Salmon is very versatile; there are as many ways to cook this fish as there are cooks. It easily accommodates elaborate preparations, but it's just as enjoyable prepared simply with lots of familiar Mediterranean flavours. **Serves 4**

2 tablespoons (30 mL) of olive oil
1 red onion, thinly sliced
4 garlic cloves, thinly sliced
2 cups (500 mL) of halved cherry tomatoes
1/2 cup (125 mL) of chopped pitted Kalamata olives
1 teaspoon (5 mL) of dried oregano
1 cup (250 mL) of orange juice
1 tablespoon (15 mL) of red wine vinegar
4 centre-cut salmon fillets (each about 6 ounces/175 g), patted dry
A sprinkle or two of salt and lots of freshly ground pepper
2 green onions, thinly sliced

In your favourite large heavy sauté pan or frying pan, heat the oil over medium-high heat. Toss in the onion and garlic and sauté for a few minutes until lightly browned, soft, and aromatic. Add the tomatoes, olives, oregano, orange juice, and vinegar; cook until simmering, a few minutes longer. Lightly season the salmon fillets to your taste with salt and pepper, then nestle them in the tomato mixture. Lower the heat so the liquid is just barely simmering, cover, and simmer until the fish is cooked through but still juicy, 10 to 15 minutes. Serve and share, with lots of the tomato mixture spooned over the salmon.

KITCHEN TIP
With a cooking method like this one, you really don't need to worry about overcooking the salmon because its juices will be absorbed by the tomato mixture and ultimately served with the fish.

MEAT

"The Chef's Steak" Grilled Rib-Eye with Tarragon Mustard Butter, 125

Grilled Flank Steak with Grilled Asparagus and Sun-Dried Tomato Pesto, 126

Grilled New York Strip Loin with Grilled Garlic and Onions, 129

Brown Butter Pan-Roasted Filet Mignon with Garlic and Thyme, 130

Beer-Braised Beef Short Ribs, 133

Italian-Style Meatloaf with Sun-Dried Tomatoes, Black Olives, Oregano, and Parmesan, 134

Mediterranean Beef Stew, 138

Curried Beef Skewers with Lime Mint Yogurt, 141

Amarone-Braised Lamb Shanks, 142

Pan-Roasted Lamb Chops with Fresh Tomato Mint Chutney, 145

Grilled Pork Chops with Grilled Bell Peppers, 146

Honey Mustard Barbecue Baked Baby Back Ribs, 149

Roasted Cherry Tomato Penne with Italian Sausage and Fresh Basil, 150

Prosciutto Roast Pork Tenderloin with Fennel Carrot Slaw, 155

Molasses Rum Grilled Pork Tenderloin with Grilled Green and Red Onions, 156

Grilled Turkey Breast with Cranberry Sage BBQ Sauce, 159

Roasted Chicken Wings, 160

Thyme-Baked Chicken with Mushroom Red Wine Sauce, 163

Coconut-Crusted Chicken with Mango Ginger Mint Salsa, 164

Grenadian Caramel Nutmeg Chicken, 167

"THE CHEF'S STEAK" GRILLED RIB-EYE WITH TARRAGON MUSTARD BUTTER

Of all the steaks that I've ever grilled, the rib-eye is by far my favourite. It's cut from the prime rib and thus beautifully marbled with fat, which of course means flavour, lots of flavour—the sort of addictive flavour that turns on a chef. And of course any steak is even better with a slice of old-school flavoured butter melting over the top. **Serves 4**

1/4 cup (60 mL) of softened butter
1 tablespoon (15 mL) of finely chopped fresh tarragon
1 tablespoon (15 mL) of minced shallot
1 tablespoon (15 mL) of Dijon mustard
1 teaspoon (5 mL) of Worcestershire sauce
4 rib-eye steaks, each 1 inch (2.5 cm) thick
Several sprinkles of salt and lots of freshly ground pepper

Begin with the flavoured butter. In a small bowl, stir together the butter, tarragon, shallot, mustard, and Worcestershire sauce. Place a roughly square piece of plastic wrap on your work surface. Scoop the butter onto the plastic wrap close to the edge nearest to you, forming a rough log about 4 inches (10 cm) long. Roll the plastic wrap around the butter once, then use your fingers to shape the butter into a smooth, even log. Tightly roll up the plastic wrap, grasp the ends of the plastic, and twirl the works a few times, tightening the butter into a perfect cylinder. Refrigerate for several hours or overnight until the butter is firm enough to slice.

Prepare and preheat your grill to its highest setting. Just before you cook them, pat the steaks dry and season them heavily with salt and pepper.

Lightly oil the grill, then place the steaks at a 45-degree angle to the grates. After a few minutes, turn them 90 degrees to get the perfect steakhouse grill marks. Grill for a few minutes longer, then flip and repeat. A medium-rare steak will take about 10 to 12 minutes in total. Serve each steak with a thick slice of steakhouse butter gently melting over the top.

KITCHEN TIP

To gauge the doneness of the steaks, poke them with your finger. As they cook, their muscle fibres tighten, so you'll feel the increased resistance as they progress in doneness. Of course this is a skill that takes some time to master, so feel free to do what every novice cook does: make a small cut into the meat and have a peek.

GRILLED FLANK STEAK WITH GRILLED ASPARAGUS AND SUN-DRIED TOMATO PESTO

In the world of meat, the more a muscle works, the tougher it gets and the more flavour it develops. But unlike most tougher cuts, flank steak does not require a long cooking time to tenderize. This cut is not quite as tender as a strip loin or rib-eye, but it is tender enough to simply grill as a way to enjoy its unmistakably deep beefy flavour. I love it with smoky charred asparagus topped with brightly flavoured sun-dried tomato pesto. **Serves 4**

FOR THE PESTO

1 cup (250 mL) of tightly packed fresh basil leaves
1/2 cup (125 mL) of oil-packed sun-dried tomatoes
1/4 cup (60 mL) of pine nuts
1/4 cup (60 mL) of grated Parmigiano-Reggiano cheese
1/4 cup (60 mL) of extra virgin olive oil

FOR THE STEAK

1 flank steak (1-1/2 to 2 pounds/750 g to 1 kg)
A sprinkle or two of salt and lots of freshly ground pepper
2 tablespoons (30 mL) of olive oil
1 bunch of asparagus (about 1 pound/500 g), woody end of the stems trimmed off

Make the pesto first. Toss the basil, tomatoes, pine nuts, Parmesan, and olive oil into your food processor. Pulse just long enough to coarsely chop and thoroughly mix the pesto, but not long enough to smoothly purée it.

Prepare and preheat your grill to its highest setting.

Season the steak well with salt and pepper to your taste. Grill the steak, turning once or twice, until it reaches your favourite doneness. Medium-rare will take about 10 minutes in total.

While the steak is grilling, splash the olive oil on the asparagus and season to your taste with salt and pepper. Place on the grill perpendicular to the grates. Grill, rolling with a pair of tongs to expose all sides to the heat, until they're tender and slightly charred, about 5 minutes. Arrange on a serving platter.

When the steak is done, let it rest for a few minutes before slicing it across the grain into very thin strips. Arrange over the asparagus and top with the pesto. Serve and share!

KITCHEN TIP

If you slice the flank steak immediately after grilling it, you'll lose quite a bit of its tasty juices. As any meat roasts, its fibres tense and its internal juices heat up and are driven to the centre, where they accumulate under pressure. Resting the meat after cooking gives the fibres a chance to relax and reabsorb the flavourful juices.

GRILLED NEW YORK STRIP LOIN WITH GRILLED GARLIC AND ONIONS

I love roasted garlic almost as much as I love grilled steak. This dish combines both addictively tasty ingredients with equally attractive grilled onions. The flavours are simple but the results are memorably flavourful. **Serves 4**

4 thick New York strip loin steaks, neatly trimmed by your butcher
A sprinkle or two of salt and lots of freshly ground pepper
4 large onions
1/4 cup (60 mL) of olive oil
4 heads of garlic

Prepare and preheat your grill to its highest setting.

Pat the steaks dry and season them lightly with salt and pepper to your taste. Neatly trim the top and bottom of the onions, then peel them. Slice each one into 4 thick slices, taking care to keep their rings intact. Neatly spread them out on a platter and brush lightly with olive oil. Lightly season to your taste with salt and pepper. Using a serrated knife, slice off the top third of each garlic head. Brush the exposed garlic with oil and season them as well.

Place the steaks on one side of your grill at a 45-degree angle to the grates. After a few minutes, turn the steaks 90 degrees to get the perfect steakhouse grill marks. Grill for a few minutes longer, then flip and repeat. A medium-rare steak will take about 10 minutes. Rest the steaks on a serving platter while the onions and garlic finish.

Meanwhile, on the other side of your grill, arrange the onion rings and garlic heads cut side down. Turn the onions once they begin to brown. Continue cooking the garlic heads until they soften and lightly brown.

Squeeze a head of grilled garlic cloves onto each steak and top with the grilled onions. Serve and share!

KITCHEN TIP
- Patting meat dry is essential before grilling. Wet meat steams on the grill, but dry meat easily develops the flavourful crusty exterior that defines a great steak.
- Grilling or roasting garlic transforms its sharp pungency into a smooth, mellow, caramelized treat.

BROWN BUTTER PAN-ROASTED FILET MIGNON WITH GARLIC AND THYME

Filet mignon is melt-in-your-mouth tender but within the world of beef comparatively bland. These steaks are at their best when their cooking method adds lots of brown flavour. That's why I love searing them in flavourful brown butter, then finishing them with aromatic thyme and pungent garlic. **Serves 4**

4 large filets mignons (each 6 to 8 ounces/175 to 250 g), patted dry
A sprinkle or two of salt and lots of freshly ground pepper
1 tablespoon (15 mL) of vegetable oil
2 tablespoons (30 mL) of butter
4 garlic cloves, minced
1 heaping tablespoon (20 mL) of minced fresh thyme

Pat the steaks dry and lightly season them with salt and pepper to your taste. Preheat your heaviest (preferably cast-iron) frying pan over medium-high heat. Splash in the vegetable oil and gently swirl it to coat the pan. Continue heating until the oil is shimmering hot but not smoking. Add the butter to the side of the pan where the oil gathers and pools. When the butter has melted, swirl the pan for a moment or two until the butter just begins to brown and sizzle. Add the steaks to the pan, arranging them slightly apart from each other. Watch and listen to the still-browning butter. Adjust the heat so it's high enough to maintain a sizzling sear but not so high that the butter begins to burn.

Sear the steaks in the butter, turning them once or twice, until they're well browned, 5 or 6 minutes or so on each side. Baste the meat constantly, angling the pan briefly and spooning some of the flavourful butter over the top of the meat, then letting it run off. Continue cooking until the steaks reach your preferred doneness: they're medium-rare when a meat thermometer inserted into them reaches 140°F (60°C), 10 to 12 minutes in total.

Rest the steaks briefly on a serving platter. Just before serving, return the pan to medium-high heat and swirl the garlic into the butter. Cook just a few moments, until sizzling and aromatic. Stir in the thyme, then immediately spoon the fragrant butter over the steaks. Serve and share!

KITCHEN TIP

Filet mignon is one of the least flavourful cuts on the cow. It's prized for its tenderness, but because it's a relatively inactive muscle, it lacks flavour. This cut benefits mightily from patient caramelization, transforming it with a prized crusty exterior and a lusciously smooth interior.

BEER-BRAISED BEEF SHORT RIBS

If you crave deep, rich beefy flavour as much as I do, then you'll love braising beef short ribs. Of all the cuts available, these have the richest, beefiest flavour. They're quite tough, though, so they need a slow, patient braising surrounded by tasty broth to release all that flavour. **Serves 4**

2 tablespoons (30 mL) of any cooking oil
4 pounds (2 kg) of beef short ribs, cut into 3- to 4-inch (8 to 10 cm) lengths
4 onions, thinly sliced
8 garlic cloves, thinly sliced
2 bottles of your favourite dark beer
1 tablespoon (15 mL) of dried thyme
2 bay leaves
A sprinkle or two of salt and lots of freshly ground pepper

Preheat your oven to 350°F (190°C).

Splash the oil into a Dutch oven or your favourite large heavy ovenproof pan with a tight-fitting lid. Over medium-high heat, patiently and thoroughly brown the ribs, about 10 minutes. For best results, don't crowd the pan—instead, brown the ribs in two batches. Transfer the ribs to a plate. Pour off most of the fat, then toss in the onions and garlic. Sauté until they're golden brown and fragrant, about 10 minutes.

Pour in the beer and stir in the thyme and bay leaves. Place the ribs on top of the onions. Season lightly with salt and pepper. Bring to a boil, then cover the pot tightly with a lid or foil. Place the works in your oven.

Braise the ribs until they're tender and the meat easily pulls away from the bones, 2 to 2-1/2 hours. Transfer the ribs and onions to a serving platter and cover with foil to keep them warm. Skim off as much fat from the braising liquid as possible, then bring it to a boil over high heat and quickly reduce it to a sauce-like consistency. Remove and discard the bay leaves. Pour the sauce over the ribs. Serve and share!

KITCHEN TIP

One of the hallmarks of any great braised or stewed beef dish is the deep, rich flavours that can come only from patiently browning the meat. This essential flavour building can happen only at the beginning; when liquid is added to the pot, the temperature drops well below the magic caramelizing zone.

ITALIAN-STYLE MEATLOAF WITH SUN-DRIED TOMATOES, BLACK OLIVES, OREGANO, AND PARMESAN

Meatloaf is easy to make, which makes it an excellent base for freestyle flavour. Cooks all over the world stir local flavours into ground meat. My favourite version comes from the grand tradition of Italian cooking. This is a great way to jazz up this old-fashioned classic with a newfangled twist or two! **Serves 4 to 6**

2 tablespoons (30 mL) of olive oil
2 large onions, finely chopped
8 garlic cloves, thinly sliced
2 large eggs
1/2 cup (125 mL) of tomato paste
1-1/2 pounds (750 g) of ground beef chuck
2 cups (500 mL) of dry bread crumbs
1/2 cup (125 mL) of chopped sun-dried tomatoes
1/2 cup (125 mL) of chopped pitted Kalamata olives
1/2 cup (125 mL) of grated Parmigiano-Reggiano cheese
1/2 cup (125 mL) of chopped fresh parsley
1 tablespoon (15 mL) of dried oregano
1 teaspoon (5 mL) of your favourite hot sauce

Preheat your oven to 350°F (190°C). Lightly oil a small baking sheet.

In your favourite sauté pan over medium-high heat, heat the olive oil, then toss in the onions and garlic. Sauté them until they're golden brown and fragrant, about 10 minutes.

Meanwhile, lightly whisk the eggs in a large bowl. Whisk in the tomato paste. Add the ground beef, bread crumbs, tomatoes, olives, Parmesan, parsley, oregano, hot sauce, and the sautéed onions. Quickly and efficiently stir and blend with your hands until everything is thoroughly mixed. Transfer to the baking sheet and shape into a thick loaf.

Bake until a meat thermometer inserted into the centre of the meatloaf reads 160°F (70°C), about 1 hour. Serve and share!

KITCHEN TIP

- Sautéing the onions first not only adds flavour to them but also removes any excess moisture that may weigh down the meatloaf.
- If possible, ask your butcher to coarsely grind the chuck meat for you; your meatloaf will have a heartier, meatier texture.

KNIVES & POTS

You don't need a chef's inventory of oddly shaped knives and obscure pots to succeed in the kitchen. For 99 percent of your day-to-day needs, just a few basic tools will do:

• One large pot, big enough to boil pasta in

• One smaller pot, big enough for a batch of pasta sauce

• One frying pan, large enough to fry up a batch of pancakes

• One large chef's knife, for the bulk of your slicing and dicing

• One serrated knife, for slicing bread

• One small paring knife, for opening envelopes and cutting limes for your gin and tonics

MEDITERRANEAN BEEF STEW

Beef stew is universal. Gently stewing and simmering tough cubes of meat into tender, flavourful submission is a common cooking method all over the world. Cooks everywhere take the opportunity to stir local flavours into the pot. The flavours of the Mediterranean are among my favourites. **Serves 4 to 6**

2 tablespoons (30 mL) of olive oil
2 pounds (1 kg) of beef stewing meat, cut into 1-inch (2.5 cm) cubes, patted dry
4 onions, sliced
8 garlic cloves, thinly sliced
1 can (28 ounces/796 mL) of chopped tomatoes
1 tablespoon (15 mL) of dried oregano
1 cup (250 mL) of Kalamata olives, pitted and halved
1 tablespoon (15 mL) of drained capers
The zest and juice of 1 lemon
1 bunch of parsley, chopped
A sprinkle or two of salt and lots of freshly ground pepper

Preheat your oven to 300°F (150°C).

Splash the oil into a Dutch oven or your favourite stew pot with a tight-fitting lid. Heat the oil over medium-high heat until it's hot but not smoking. Patiently brown the beef in several batches, taking care not to crowd the pot. Adjust the heat as needed to keep the meat sizzling and browning. Transfer each batch of the browned meat to a plate. After you've removed the last batch of meat, toss in the onions and garlic and sauté until they're golden brown and aromatic, about 10 minutes.

Return the browned beef to the pot. Stir in the tomatoes and oregano. Bring to a boil, then cover tightly and transfer to your oven. Continue cooking, stirring occasionally, until the meat is tender, about 1 hour. A few minutes before serving, stir in the olives, capers, lemon zest, lemon juice, parsley, and salt and pepper to your taste. Serve and share!

KITCHEN TIP

Instead of stewing the meat in the oven, you may continue simmering it on top of your stove. Adjust the heat so the aromatic stewing liquid is just barely simmering. Alternatively, after you brown the meat, you may pour everything into your slow cooker and simmer for a few hours until tender.

CURRIED BEEF SKEWERS WITH LIME MINT YOGURT

On the street corners of the world, ground beef is grilled in many ways—juicy hamburger patties, spicy seasoned tacos, even hand-formed skewers. For cooks all over the globe, ground beef is dressed up with local aromatic flavours. I enjoyed this favourite on my first trip to Greece. **Serves 4**

1 egg
4 garlic cloves, minced
1 tablespoon (15 mL) of dried oregano
1 tablespoon (15 mL) of curry powder
1 tablespoon (15 mL) of tomato paste
1 pound (500 g) of ground beef chuck
A sprinkle or two of salt and lots of freshly ground pepper
Olive oil for drizzling

FOR THE DIPPING SAUCE

The zest and juice of 1 lime
1/2 cup (125 mL) of plain yogurt
1/2 cup (125 mL) of finely chopped fresh mint

Soak 8 long wooden skewers in a bowl of water for an hour or so. Prepare and preheat your grill to its highest setting.

In a medium bowl, gently whisk together the egg, garlic, oregano, curry powder, and tomato paste. Add the ground meat and lightly season it to your taste with salt and pepper. Mix everything together quickly and efficiently with your hands. Divide the mixture into 8 parts and carefully form each portion into a thick cigar shape around the top 6 inches (15 cm) or so of a wooden skewer. Drizzle the skewers with olive oil and reserve on a platter.

Stir the lime zest, lime juice, yogurt, and mint together to make a simple dipping sauce.

Grill the skewers, turning frequently, until they're nicely browned, juicy, and tender, 6 to 8 minutes. Serve and share with the dipping sauce.

KITCHEN TIP

- It's best to avoid overmixing the ground meat—its texture is best when it remains a bit coarse.
- The structure of cooked ground beef is very strong, so it easily absorbs many creative ingredients and flavours. As with any ground meat, though, if the meat is accidentally overcooked, the oven or grill's heat will first squeeze out all its juicy, flavourful moisture before the protein structure literally breaks down and crumbles into oblivion.

AMARONE-BRAISED LAMB SHANKS

Lamb shanks are an essential part of any cook's repertoire. They're intensely flavourful and also inexpensive. They do need a long, slow braising to fully tenderize, but they'll reward your patience with a richly flavoured meaty and memorable meal. I think of them as a special-occasion treat, which is why I find it so easy to pour an entire bottle of one of the world's great wines into the pot! **Serves 4**

2 or 3 tablespoons (30 or 45 mL) of olive oil
4 large lamb shanks
2 onions, diced
2 carrots, diced
8 garlic cloves, thinly sliced
2 bay leaves
2 large sprigs of rosemary
1 can (5-1/2 ounces/156 mL) of tomato paste
1 bottle of Amarone or other big, flavourful red wine
A sprinkle or two of salt and lots of freshly ground pepper
1/2 cup (125 mL) of chopped fresh parsley

Preheat your oven to 300°F (150°C).

Splash the olive oil into a Dutch oven or your favourite soup pot and heat it over medium-high heat. Add the shanks and brown them thoroughly, turning once or twice until all the sides are golden brown and caramelized. Transfer the shanks to a plate.

Add the onions, carrots, and garlic to the pot and sauté until the vegetables soften and brown lightly, about 10 minutes. Toss in the bay leaves and rosemary, spoon in the tomato paste, and pour in the wine. Stir everything together, then nestle the lamb shanks into the works. Bring the liquid to a boil, then cover tightly and transfer to your oven. Braise until the meat is tender, about 90 minutes.

Carefully transfer the shanks to a platter, cover them with foil, and keep them warm in the oven while you finish the sauce. Place the pot over medium-high heat and boil until the braising broth reduces to a sauce-like consistency, about 5 minutes. Stir in the parsley and pour the sauce over the lamb shanks. Serve and share!

KITCHEN TIP

- Lamb shanks are full of connective tissue that dissolves in the braising liquid during the cooking, giving the sauce a beautiful silky smooth texture.
- Amarone is made from partially sun-dried grapes, so it has an intense raisin-like flavour that easily and extravagantly flavours the rich, hearty lamb shanks.

PAN-ROASTED LAMB CHOPS WITH FRESH TOMATO MINT CHUTNEY

I love the rustic flavour of juicy lamb chops, especially topped with spoonfuls of a bright condiment like this chutney, which features sweet cherry tomatoes quickly stewed with sweet brown sugar, sour red wine vinegar, aromatic spices, and a last-second fresh mint accent. **Serves 4**

FOR THE TOMATO CHUTNEY

1 tablespoon (15 mL) of red wine vinegar
2 green onions, white and green parts thinly sliced separately
1 tablespoon (15 mL) of brown sugar
1/2 teaspoon (5 mL) of your favourite hot sauce
1/2 teaspoon (2 mL) of ground cloves
1/2 teaspoon (2 mL) of salt
2 cups (500 mL) of cherry tomatoes, halved
1/2 cup (125 mL) of chopped fresh mint

8 lamb loin chops
A sprinkle or two of salt and lots of freshly ground pepper
1/4 cup (60 mL) of vegetable oil

To make the chutney, pour the vinegar into a medium saucepan. Add the white part of the green onions, the sugar, hot sauce, cloves, and salt. Bring to a quick simmer for a minute or two. Stir in the tomatoes and cook just long enough for the mixture to again simmer. Transfer to a serving bowl and stir in the mint and green tops of the onions, preserving their fresh flavour.

Preheat your favourite heavy frying pan over medium-high heat.

Pat the lamb chops dry on folded paper towels and season them to your taste with salt and pepper. Pour half the oil into the pan, gently swirling to evenly coat the bottom. Wait for the oil to heat through. Gauge its temperature by holding a chop with a pair of tongs and tentatively dipping in one corner. If it doesn't sizzle dramatically, wait a few moments until the oil is hotter.

Place as many of the chops in the pan as you can without crowding them and slowing down the heat. You can always brown a few in a second batch with the remaining oil if you need to. Sear the chops, turning once, until medium-rare, 4 or 5 minutes per side. Serve and share with the tomato chutney.

KITCHEN TIP

Lamb chops are built for speed. They're cut from the loin, so their meat is tender, and with just a quick heating, they're ready to go. They're low in fat too, which means they require quick cooking. Too long in the pan and they'll lose what little flavourful juicy fat they have and quickly dry out. A hot pan is key. Browning starts immediately and finishes before the interior overcooks.

GRILLED PORK CHOPS WITH GRILLED BELL PEPPERS

Pork chops are perfect for the grill. Their lean white flesh is easy to brown and easily absorbs the smoky essence of the grill. While the grill is fiery hot, bring a medley of bell peppers along for a flavour ride too!
Serves 4

4 bone-in pork rib chops, about 1-inch (2.5 cm) thick
1 red bell pepper, quartered and seeded
1 green bell pepper, quartered and seeded
1 yellow bell pepper, quartered and seeded
A splash or two of vegetable oil
A sprinkle or two of salt and lots of freshly ground pepper
A drizzle or two of balsamic vinegar

Rest the pork chops at room temperature for 20 minutes or so before cooking. Ready the peppers for the grill by gently flattening them, then gently tossing them with a splash of vegetable oil. Lightly season them to your taste with salt and pepper.

Prepare and preheat your grill to its highest setting.

Pat the pork chops dry, then rub them with a splash of vegetable oil. Season them lightly to your taste with salt and pepper. Grill, turning once or twice, until a meat thermometer inserted in the centre registers 145°F (65°C), about 10 minutes.

Meanwhile, place the bell peppers on the grill and sear until tender, turning once or twice. Top each pork chop with some of the grilled peppers and drizzle with balsamic vinegar. Serve and share!

KITCHEN TIP
Because pork is so lean, it can dry out very quickly on the grill. Bringing the meat to room temperature before grilling shortens the amount of time the meat has to spend on the grill before it's properly cooked. The exterior doesn't dry out waiting for the centre to cook through.

HONEY MUSTARD BARBECUE BAKED BABY BACK RIBS

The secret to great-tasting ribs infused with barbecue flavour and so tender they're falling off the bone is time—lots of it. Ribs are incredibly tough, so it takes long, slow, patient cooking to coax out their flavour and render them tender. A brightly flavoured barbecue sauce doesn't hurt either! **Serves 4**

2 racks of baby back ribs
1 cup (250 mL) of orange juice
1/2 cup (125 mL) of honey
1/2 cup (125 mL) of yellow mustard
1/2 cup (125 mL) of ketchup
1/2 cup (125 mL) of cider vinegar
2 tablespoons (30 mL) of Worcestershire sauce
1 tablespoon (15 mL) of soy sauce
1 teaspoon (5 mL) of your favourite hot sauce

Preheat your oven to 300°F (150°C).

Arrange the ribs in a large roasting pan or baking dish. Whisk together the remaining ingredients and pour over the ribs, turning the meat once or twice to evenly coat it. Cover the pan as tightly as possible with foil.

Bake the ribs for 3 hours. Remove the foil and continue baking for another hour, turning the ribs a few times to baste them with the flavourful barbecue sauce.

Arrange the ribs on a serving platter. Pour off any fat that has accumulated with the sauce and pour the sauce over the ribs. Serve and share!

KITCHEN TIP

Because of the long cooking time, it is important that no moisture escapes from the pan—if it does, the ribs will eventually dry out. If your pan is wider than your foil, you can fashion two sheets into one larger one. Lay one sheet directly on top of a second sheet. Carefully and tightly fold one long edge over twice, about 1 inch (2.5 cm) each time. Open up the two sheets like a book, flatten and crease the middle seam with your finger, then tightly cover the pan. You'll have plenty of foil to tightly crimp the edges and protect the ribs during their slow, moist braise.

ROASTED CHERRY TOMATO PENNE WITH ITALIAN SAUSAGE AND FRESH BASIL

Every day, chefs bring out a wide range of flavours on the job. Few of those flavours seem to make it home, though. This deeply flavourful pasta dish is one that has. Long ago in a restaurant kitchen I discovered that slowly roasting a pan of fresh tomatoes with Italian sausage transformed the mix into an intensely flavoured rustic pasta sauce. Cooks' food. Crew lunch. An old friend! **Serves 4**

8 cups (2 L) of cherry tomatoes
1 large onion, thinly sliced
4 garlic cloves, thinly sliced
4 Italian sausages, sliced into 1/2-inch (1 cm) thick rounds
2 tablespoons (30 mL) of olive oil
A sprinkle or two of salt and lots of freshly ground pepper
12 ounces (375 g) of penne
Leaves from 1 large bunch of fresh basil
4 green onions

Preheat your oven to 400°F (200°C).

Toss the tomatoes, onions, garlic, sausages, and olive oil together. Season to your taste with salt and pepper. Transfer to a roasting pan and place in the oven. Roast until the tomatoes, onion, and sausages are lightly brown and smell amazing, 30 to 45 minutes.

When the tomatoes are nearly done, bring a large pot of salted water to a full rolling boil. Dump in the penne and cook until edible, stirring occasionally. After 10 minutes or so fish out a piece and bite it. At first it will be too firm, but in just a few minutes it will transform, so continue fishing and tasting until you like the texture. Pasta is best when it's tender enough to eat but hasn't become too soft. Great pasta retains lots of pleasing chewy texture.

While the pasta is cooking, stack a tall pile of basil leaves, roll it into a tight cylinder, and slice as thinly as possible. Slice the green onions as well.

As the pasta finishes cooking, add a ladleful of the pasta water to the roasting pan. The moisture will dissolve any caramelized brown bits of flavour on the bottom of the pan. When the pasta is done, drain it and return it to the pot. Add the roasted sausages, onions, and tomatoes, scraping along every last bit of roasted flavour from the pan. Toss in the basil leaves and green onions and stir everything together. Serve and share!

KITCHEN TIP

Busy restaurant cooks pay no attention to the clock. They simply watch their food. Keep an eye on it. Make decisions. Watch for flavour. Wait for flavour. Stay vigilant and patient. The dissolving tomatoes and browning sausage will reward you with a deeply flavoured rustic pasta dish.

TIME AND DONENESS

"How long until it's done?" That's certainly one of the most common questions in any kitchen.

In most recipes, timing is portrayed as rigid and precise. But timing is actually one of the most flexible factors in your kitchen. It's affected by numerous variables, many beyond your control. Words on paper cannot replace the in-the-moment accuracy of your own observations. For instance, regardless of how it gets there, a roast chicken is done when it reaches 165°F (72°C) internally.

So perhaps a better question is "How do I know *when* it's done?"

PROSCIUTTO ROAST PORK TENDERLOIN WITH FENNEL CARROT SLAW

This dish shows off a neat prosciutto party trick. Thin slices of this special cured meat are easily wrapped around just about any meat or fish. When heated, even over a wet marinade, the prosciutto slices will shrink-wrap and bind, holding on tightly in a way that other hams don't. **Serves 4 to 6**

6 thin slices of prosciutto
2 pork tenderloins (each 8 to 12 ounces/250 to 375 g), trimmed and patted dry

FOR THE SLAW

2 tablespoons (30 mL) of white wine vinegar
2 tablespoons (30 mL) of honey
2 tablespoons (30 mL) of olive oil
1 tablespoon (15 mL) of dried dill
1 cup (250 mL) of grated fennel bulb
1/2 cup (125 mL) of grated carrot
1 red onion, thinly sliced
A sprinkle or two of salt and lots of freshly ground pepper

Preheat your oven to 375°F (190°C).

Lay a prosciutto slice on your work surface with a narrow side facing you. Lay another slice to the side, overlapping the first by half or so. Add a third, again overlapping by half. Fold under several inches of the narrow tapered end of a tenderloin, so the loin is an even thickness along its length and the same width as the overlapping prosciutto. Place the pork tenderloin along the bottom edge of the prosciutto slices and roll the meats into a tight cylinder. Place the loin seam side down in a roasting pan or on a baking sheet. Repeat with the remaining prosciutto and tenderloin. Roast until a meat thermometer reads between 160°F and 170°F (70°C to 75°C), 15 to 20 minutes. Let rest a few minutes.

Meanwhile, make the slaw. Whisk together the vinegar, honey, olive oil, and dill into a smooth dressing. Add the fennel, carrots, and onion. Toss everything together until the veggies are coated well with the dressing. Slice the tenderloins into a few thick pieces. Serve and share with the slaw.

KITCHEN TIP

Pork tenderloin is available in various trimmed forms. Ask your butcher to remove the "silverskin," a tough connective tissue covering the thicker end of the meat.

MOLASSES RUM GRILLED PORK TENDERLOIN WITH GRILLED GREEN AND RED ONIONS

Pork tenderloins are excellent for grilling. They easily absorb aromatic marinade flavours and then the flavours of your grill. Today's pork is relatively lean, so it benefits from a fast sear on your grill. High heat browns the meat before the interior overcooks and dries out. While the grill is running at full throttle, it's easy to toss on a few onions too. They automatically taste good with anything grilled. **Serves 4**

1/2 cup (125 mL) of molasses
1/4 cup (60 mL) of spiced rum
2 tablespoons (30 mL) of grainy mustard
1 tablespoon (15 mL) of soy sauce
1 teaspoon (5 mL) of ground allspice
1 teaspoon (5 mL) of your favourite hot sauce
2 pork tenderloins (each 8 to 12 ounces/250 to 375 g), trimmed and patted dry
2 large red onions, thickly sliced
4 green onions
A good drizzle of olive oil
A sprinkle or two of salt and lots of freshly ground pepper

Stir the molasses, rum, mustard, soy sauce, allspice, and hot sauce together. Place the pork in a resealable plastic bag, then pour in the marinade. Massage with your fingers, evenly distributing the flavour. Marinate for at least 1 hour or refrigerate overnight for maximum flavour.

Prepare and preheat your grill to its highest setting.

Arrange the red onions on a baking sheet, carefully keeping the rings intact. Lay the green onions next to each other on the same sheet. Drizzle them all lightly with olive oil and season them with salt and pepper to your taste.

Remove the tenderloins from the marinade, discarding the marinade. Place the tenderloins diagonally across the grates of the grill. Grill, turning once or twice, until a meat thermometer inserted into the thickest part of the meat reads between 160°F and 170°F (70°C to 75°C), 15 to 20 minutes. Transfer the pork to a serving platter, loosely tent with foil, and let rest for a few minutes, giving it a chance to reabsorb its juices.

Meanwhile, carefully position the green onions perpendicular to the grates, and carefully place the red onions next to them. Grill until lightly browned, about 10 minutes on each side.

Slice the pork and arrange on plates or a platter. Scatter both kinds of onions over the sliced pork. Serve and share!

KITCHEN TIP
Under pressure from the high heat of the grill penetrating from the exterior, the delicate juices of pork tenderloin (or any meat, for that matter) concentrate in the meat's centre. If the meat isn't allowed to rest before it's sliced, those juices are released, squeezed out by tense meat fibres, to pool on your plate. Resting allows the heat-stressed meat fibres to relax and to reabsorb the flavourful juices.

GRILLED TURKEY BREAST WITH CRANBERRY SAGE BBQ SAUCE

You can do a lot more with turkey than just roast a giant one once a year with holiday gravy. Now and then during the rest of the year, bring home a simple boneless turkey breast and grill it. You'll enjoy the smoky flavours of roast turkey without the hassles of the oven. And you can still have cranberry too! **Serves 4**

1/4 cup (60 mL) of vegetable oil
1 tablespoon (15 mL) of chili powder
1 tablespoon (15 mL) of cinnamon
1 teaspoon (5 mL) of salt
1 teaspoon (5 mL) of your favourite hot sauce
A boneless skinless half turkey breast (2 to 3 pounds/1 to 1.5 kg), patted dry

FOR THE BARBECUE SAUCE

1 cup (250 mL) of cranberry jelly
2 tablespoons (30 mL) of Dijon mustard
2 tablespoons (30 mL) of olive oil
1 tablespoon (15 mL) of crumbled dried sage
1 tablespoon (15 mL) of chili powder
1 tablespoon (15 mL) of soy sauce

Prepare and preheat your grill to medium.

Whisk together the olive oil, chili powder, cinnamon, salt, and hot sauce. Rub the aromatic oil all over the turkey breast. Place the turkey on your grill. Close the lid and begin roasting, turning every 10 minutes or so.

While the turkey is grilling, whip up the barbecue sauce. In a small bowl, whisk together the cranberry jelly, mustard, olive oil, sage, chili powder, and soy sauce.

After 30 minutes or so, when the turkey has begun to brown, begin brushing on the barbecue sauce. Add another coat every few minutes, turning the meat over as you do.

The turkey is done when a meat thermometer inserted in its thickest part reads 165°F (72°C), about an hour in total. Transfer the breast to a serving platter to rest for 15 minutes or so. Drizzle on any extra barbecue sauce. Serve and share!

KITCHEN TIP

Because the cranberry jelly in the barbecue sauce is loaded with sugar, it will burn if exposed to too much heat. That's why it's best to glaze with the sauce as the turkey finishes, toward the end of its cooking time.

ROASTED CHICKEN WINGS

You don't need a deep-fryer to enjoy chicken wings at home. They're just as tasty tossed with an aromatic herb coating and simply roasted. Caramelized chicken always tastes good! **Serves 4 to 6**

2 tablespoons (30 mL) of whole wheat flour
2 tablespoons (30 mL) of sugar
1 tablespoon (15 mL) of dried thyme
2 teaspoons (10 mL) of black pepper
1 teaspoon (5 mL) of salt
48 large chicken wing pieces (3 to 4 pounds/1.5 to 2 kg)

Preheat your oven to 450°F (230°C). Lightly oil 1 or 2 baking sheets.

In a large bowl, whisk together the flour, sugar, thyme, pepper, and salt. Add the wings and toss until they're evenly coated with the flour mixture. Spread the wings out in a single layer on the baking sheets. Roast, turning once after 10 minutes or so, until cooked through and golden brown, 15 to 20 minutes. Serve and share!

KITCHEN TIP
Flour and sugar speed up the browning of the wings. They help the surface brown quickly, before the chicken dries out, and add lots of toasted flavours to the roasting effort.

THYME-BAKED CHICKEN
WITH MUSHROOM RED WINE SAUCE

This is a classic group of flavours that any cook coming up the ranks in a French-inspired kitchen will learn. I never tire of the hearty flavour of thyme-scented roast chicken with earthy mushrooms and aromatic red wine. **Serves 4**

4 large boneless skinless chicken breasts
2 tablespoons (30 mL) of olive oil
1 tablespoon (15 mL) of dried thyme
A sprinkle or two of salt and lots of freshly ground pepper

FOR THE SAUCE

2 tablespoons (30 mL) of butter
8 ounces (250 g) of thinly sliced mushrooms
1 onion, chopped
2 garlic cloves, minced
1 cup (250 mL) of chicken broth
1/2 cup (125 mL) of your favourite dry red wine
1 tablespoon (15 mL) of water
1 teaspoon (5 mL) of cornstarch
2 tablespoons (30 mL) or so of chopped fresh parsley

Preheat your oven to 450°F (230°C).

Pat the chicken breasts dry with folded paper towel. Toss them into a bowl and splash in the oil. Toss until evenly coated, then evenly sprinkle on the thyme. Lightly season to your taste with salt and pepper. Arrange in a baking dish and bake until cooked through but still juicy, about 25 minutes. The chicken is perfectly cooked when a meat thermometer inserted in its thickest part reads 165°F (72°C).

Meanwhile, create the sauce. In your favourite sauté pan or frying pan, melt the butter over medium-high heat until it sizzles and lightly browns. Toss in the mushrooms, onion, and garlic and sauté until lightly browned and deliciously caramelized, 15 minutes or so. Pour in the broth and the wine and bring to a rapid simmer for a few minutes. Whisk together the water and cornstarch, then pour the slurry into the sauce, stirring gently until the sauce is evenly thickened. Remove from the heat and stir in the parsley. Season to your taste with salt and pepper. Serve with the chicken and share!

KITCHEN TIP

Cornstarch thickens hot liquids quickly, but if it continues to simmer it will lose strength over time. The molecular bonds that it initially forms to thicken the sauce will fracture and break, leaving the sauce watery. The key is to add the cornstarch just before serving, then take it off the heat.

COCONUT-CRUSTED CHICKEN WITH MANGO GINGER MINT SALSA

Crusting is a time-honoured way to jazz up just about any meat or fish by enclosing it with flavour and texture. Coconut ranks as an ideal crusting candidate, especially on chicken breasts. Its distinctive crunchy texture adheres easily to the meat while its sweet island taste inspires a simple tasty salsa. **Serves 4**

FOR THE SALSA

1 large ripe mango, peeled and diced
2 green onions, thinly sliced
1/2 cup (125 mL) of finely chopped red bell pepper
1/2 cup (125 mL) of mint sprigs, tightly stacked, rolled, and thinly sliced
The zest and juice of 1 lime
1 tablespoon (15 mL) of grated frozen ginger
1 tablespoon (15 mL) of honey
1 teaspoon (5 mL) of olive oil
1/4 teaspoon (1 mL) of salt

1 cup (250 mL) of all-purpose flour
2 eggs, lightly whisked
2 cups (500 mL) of flaked or shredded coconut, sweetened or unsweetened
A sprinkle or two of salt and lots of freshly ground pepper
4 large boneless skinless chicken breasts, trimmed and patted dry

Make the salsa first by simply tossing together the mango, green onions, red pepper, mint, lime zest, lime juice, ginger, honey, olive oil, and salt. Reserve.

Preheat your oven to 400°F (200°C). Lightly oil a baking sheet.

Put the flour, eggs, and coconut into 3 separate bowls. Season the flour. Working with one breast at a time, dredge the chicken in the flour, coating it evenly and shaking off any excess. Dip the chicken into the egg, coating it evenly and letting any excess drip off. Finally, dip the chicken into the coconut, turning, pressing, and sprinkling as needed so the crust adheres. Place the crusted breast on the baking sheet. Repeat with the remaining chicken. Bake until the breasts are golden brown and crusty, 15 to 20 minutes. The chicken is done when a meat thermometer inserted in its thickest part registers 160°F (70°C). Arrange on a serving platter and top with the salsa. Serve and share!

KITCHEN TIP

Sometimes your fingers end up just as crusty as the food you're breading. To minimize mess and avoid thick fingers, it helps to designate one hand for wet, the other for dry. As you bread the breasts, they'll alternately be wet then dry. If you only touch wet with your wet hand and dry with your dry hand, your fingers will stay manageable.

GRENADIAN CARAMEL NUTMEG CHICKEN

As a wandering chef I've enjoyed many distinctive flavours around the world. One of my favourites is this uniquely prepared dish. It's remarkably simple and full of authentic island flavour. The unusual cooking method slowly caramelizes and tenderizes the chicken, simmering it in—and infusing it with—a fragrant nutmeg broth. **Serves 4**

1 large chicken (about 4 pounds/2 kg)
1 cup (250 mL) of brown rice
A sprinkle or two of salt and lots of freshly ground pepper
1/2 cup (125 mL) of vegetable oil
1/2 cup (125 mL) of sugar
1 cup (250 mL) of dark spiced rum
1 tablespoon (15 mL) of freshly grated nutmeg

Cut the chicken into 10 parts (or ask your butcher to do it for you): cut each of the 2 breasts into 2 pieces, plus 2 thighs, 2 drumsticks, and 2 wings.

Make the rice first. Add the rice to a small saucepan. Pour in 2 cups (500 mL) of water and lightly season to your taste with salt and pepper. Bring to a boil over medium-high heat, then reduce the heat so the liquid is barely simmering. Cover tightly and simmer until the rice is moist and tender and has absorbed the liquid, about 45 minutes. The rice can rest for 10 or 15 minutes before serving.

While the rice is cooking, begin the chicken. Splash the oil into a heavy Dutch oven or soup pot over medium-high heat. Gently swirl the pot, coating the bottom evenly. Pour the sugar into the centre of the oil. Stir gently as the oil heats and the sugar dissolves and begins to brown. In a few minutes the colour will begin deepening. When it's a rich, fragrant golden brown, add the chicken pieces. Pour in 2 cups (500 mL) of water, the rum, and nutmeg. Stir everything together gently until the caramel dissolves and the broth boils. Lower the heat until the liquid is just barely simmering, then cover the pot with a tight-fitting lid. Simmer the chicken in the aromatic broth, without turning, until it is juicy and tender. As the stew simmers, the liquid will reduce and its flavours will concentrate. In 45 minutes or so, the broth will become a finishing sauce that beautifully glazes the chicken.

Ladle the chicken over the rice. Serve and share!

KITCHEN TIP

- Caramelizing sugar in the stew pot is an old cookhouse trick—it adds rich colour, savoury aroma, and just a little sweetness.
- Caramelized sugar tastes best when it's deep golden brown. Adding the chicken pieces will lower the temperature of the oil and sugar so they don't darken further and scorch.

VEGETABLES, GRAINS, AND SIDES

APPLE PIE BROWN RICE

The rich, earthy flavour and whole grain goodness of brown rice are an excellent base for many aromatic rice dishes. In this dish, as the rice cooks it slowly absorbs the familiar flavours of warm apple pie—an unexpected and delicious combination. **Serves 4**

2 tablespoons (30 mL) of butter
1 large onion, diced
4 garlic cloves, thinly sliced
1 teaspoon (5 mL) of cinnamon
1 teaspoon (5 mL) of dried thyme
1 large apple or 2 smaller ones, cored and chopped
1 cup (250 mL) of raisins
1 cup (250 mL) of brown rice, rinsed and drained
3-1/2 cups (875 mL) of water or chicken broth
A sprinkle or two of salt and lots of freshly ground pepper

Preheat your oven to 350°F (190°C).

Toss the butter into a small ovenproof saucepan over medium-high heat and gently swirl as it melts and begins to brown. When the butter is golden brown and fragrant, stir in the onion, garlic, and cinnamon. Continue stirring until the onion softens and begin to brown, 10 minutes or so. Stir in the apples, raisins, thyme, rice, and water. Season to your taste with salt and pepper. Bring to a boil, then cover with a tight-fitting lid and place in the oven. Bake until the rice is tender and fragrant, 60 to 70 minutes. Serve and share!

KITCHEN TIP

Like most spices, the flavour of cinnamon benefits from the short, high heat of its initial sauté before its longer, much lower, and gentler simmer. The first heat removes any storage staleness while giving the butterfat a chance to absorb and release a range of aromatic flavours in the spice that can dissolve only in fat, not water or alcohol.

CURRIED COUSCOUS
WITH CHICKPEAS AND RAISINS

Couscous is very easy to cook. It's a form of pasta, but it's much easier to prepare. It's simply stirred into hot water and allowed to stand for a few minutes. That's it. It rapidly softens, and best of all it easily absorbs whatever flavours are along for the ride. **Serves 4**

2 tablespoons (30 mL) of olive oil
1 large onion, chopped
4 garlic cloves, thinly sliced
1 tablespoon (15 mL) of curry powder
1 can (14 ounces/398 mL) of chickpeas, rinsed and drained
1 cup (250 mL) of raisins
1 cup (250 mL) of grated carrots
2 cups (500 mL) of chicken broth or water
A sprinkle or two of salt and lots of freshly ground pepper
1 cup (250 mL) of couscous

Splash the olive oil into your favourite medium saucepan over medium-high heat. When it's hot, toss in the onions, garlic, and curry powder and sauté until the onion is soft and fragrant, about 5 minutes. Stir in the chickpeas, raisins, carrots, and broth. Season with salt and pepper to your taste. Bring to a full boil, then stir in the couscous. Cover tightly, remove from the heat, and let rest until the couscous absorbs the liquid and softens, about 10 minutes. Serve and share!

KITCHEN TIP
Couscous is made from small, grainy bits of durum semolina dough, the same flour used to make pasta, but unlike pasta, couscous is already cooked. It's steamed then dried before it reaches your kitchen. It simply needs to rehydrate—to soften in water—which takes only a few minutes.

QUINOA TABBOULEH
WITH CUCUMBER AND MINT

This dish is an excellent way to show off the nutritional powerhouse quinoa in a classic healthy salad. Tabbouleh is a Middle Eastern whole grain salad traditionally made with bulgur wheat. It tastes so cool and refreshing that sometimes I make this version, using nutritious quinoa instead. Traditional chopped parsley, cool cucumber, aromatic mint, and a simple fragrant lemon dressing accent this classic group of healthful flavours. **Serves 4**

1 cup (250 mL) of quinoa
2 cups (500 mL) of water
The zest and juice of 2 lemons
1/4 cup (60 mL) of your finest olive oil
1 large cucumber, peeled, halved, seeded, and chopped
2 green onions, thinly sliced
2 cups (500 mL) of chopped fresh parsley
1 cup (250 mL) of finely chopped fresh mint leaves
A sprinkle or two of salt and lots of freshly ground pepper

Rinse the quinoa well in a strainer with lots of cold water. In a small saucepan, bring the measured water to a full boil, then reduce the heat so the liquid is barely simmering. Add the quinoa, cover, and cook until the quinoa absorbs the liquid and is tender, 15 to 20 minutes. Remove from the heat and let the quinoa stand, covered, for another 5 minutes or so.

Meanwhile, in a festive serving bowl whisk together the lemon zest, lemon juice, and olive oil. Fluff the quinoa with a fork, then add to the dressing along with the cucumber, green onions, parsley, and mint. Season to your taste with salt and pepper and toss everything together. Serve and share!

KITCHEN TIP
Quinoa is actually a seed. In nature it protects itself from ravenous birds with a discouraging bitter coating, but fortunately for humans that coating easily rinses off in water. In fact, most is long gone by the time it reaches your kitchen, but some may linger. Hence the necessary rinsing.

SAUSAGE AND PEPPER POLENTA WITH OREGANO AND RICOTTA

In many parts of northern Italy, polenta has been a staple far longer than pasta, maybe because it's just as easy to stir cornmeal into hot water as it is to throw in a handful of pasta. It's also easy to enjoy the rustic hearty flavour of what is in essence a simple savoury corn pudding. **Serves 6 to 8**

2 tablespoons (30 mL) of olive oil
4 Italian sausages, cut into large chunks
1 large onion, diced
6 garlic cloves, thinly sliced
1 red bell pepper, seeded and sliced
1 green bell pepper, seeded and sliced
4 cups (1 L) of water
1 cup (250 mL) of yellow cornmeal
1 tablespoon (15 mL) of dried oregano
1 cup (250 mL) of ricotta cheese
A sprinkle or two of salt and lots of freshly ground pepper
2 green onions, thinly sliced

Preheat your oven to 400°F (200°C). Lightly oil a medium baking dish.

Splash the olive oil into your favourite large saucepan over medium-high heat. When it's hot, toss in the sausages and sauté until cooked through and lightly browned, about 5 minutes. Transfer the sausages to a bowl. Add the onions, garlic, and red and green peppers to the pot and sauté a few minutes, until the aromatic vegetables soften and brighten. Add the veggies to the sausages.

Add the water to the pot and bring it to a boil, then reduce the heat so it just barely simmers. Whisk in the cornmeal and oregano, breaking up any lumps, and then simmer, stirring frequently with a wooden spoon, until the polenta thickens and begins to pull away from the sides of the pot, about 20 minutes.

Stir the sausage and pepper mixture into the polenta. Stir in the ricotta. Season the mixture to your taste with salt and pepper. Pour the polenta into the baking dish. Bake until the polenta sets further and lightly browns, about 20 minutes. Sprinkle with the green onions. Serve and share!

KITCHEN TIP
As polenta cooks, the ground corn granules absorb liquid, swelling and softening. In this recipe there are four parts of liquid for every one part of cornmeal. Some polenta recipes call for more cornmeal, often a three-to-one ratio. The polenta thickens faster if you add more cornmeal, but there won't be enough moisture to go around, so the finished texture will be noticeably coarser.

SWEET POTATO RISOTTO WITH CRISPY PROSCIUTTO AND SAGE

I love patiently stirring together a fresh, creamy batch of simple plain risotto, and can never resist adding in lots of aromatic flavour. This version is one of my favourites, maybe because I love the healthy flavour of sweet potatoes so much. **Serves 4**

8 cups (2 L) of chicken broth or water
1 large sweet potato, peeled and grated
4 ounces (125 g) of thinly sliced prosciutto
2 tablespoons (30 mL) of olive oil
2 onions, minced
4 garlic cloves, minced
2 cups (500 mL) of arborio, Carnaroli, or other risotto rice
1/2 cup (125 mL) of dry white wine
A sprinkle or two of salt and lots of freshly ground pepper
1 heaping cup (275 mL) of grated Grana Padano cheese
1 cup (250 mL) or so of chopped fresh parsley
1/4 cup (60 mL) or so of thinly sliced fresh sage, or 2 tablespoons (30 mL) of crumbled dried sage

Pour the chicken broth into a saucepan, then add the sweet potato. Bring to a boil, then reduce the heat until the liquid is barely simmering. Meanwhile, stack the prosciutto slices on top of each other and roll from a narrow end into a tight cylinder. Slice crosswise into thin ribbons.

Splash the olive oil into a medium saucepan over medium-high heat. When it's hot, add the prosciutto and sauté until crispy, about 5 minutes. Transfer to paper towels to drain. Add the onions and garlic to the pot and sauté until they're golden brown and fragrant, about 5 minutes.

Stir in the rice and cook, stirring constantly, until the grains are well coated with oil and slightly toasted, about 3 minutes. Keep an eye on the rice grains—they'll transform from pure white to almost entirely opaque. This step will help them stay distinct in the finished dish.

Pour in the wine, stirring as it's quickly absorbed by the rice. Lower the heat, then begin adding the simmering sweet potato broth, a cup (250 mL) or so at a time. Stir constantly, allowing each addition of the liquid to be absorbed by the rice before adding more. Continue adding broth and stirring until all the broth has been used, then begin tasting the rice grains to judge their doneness. Risotto is done when the rice grains are creamy and tender yet still firm and distinct, about 20 minutes. Season to your taste with salt and pepper. At the last second stir in the cheese, parsley, and sage. Sprinkle the crispy prosciutto on top. Serve and share!

KITCHEN TIP

Risotto owes its characteristic creaminess to several factors. It's traditionally made from varieties of rice with a very high starch content. Its distinctive cooking method gently coaxes those vital starches out of each rice grain. Because the broth is already hot, the temperature of the rice also stays consistently hot, and this along with the constant stirring encourage the release of the starch from the rice. The starch thickens the surrounding liquid, giving the dish its characteristic creamy smooth texture.

CURRIED COCONUT SPINACH

Creamed spinach is universal. All over the world, cooks cream hearty, healthy green leaves with lots of local flavour, and throughout Southeast Asia and India that often means coconut milk and local curry. This deceptively simple version is packed with aromatic flavour and much lighter than Old World cream and butter. **Serves 4**

1 can (14 ounces/400 mL) of coconut milk

1 or 2 teaspoons (5 or 10 mL) of yellow, green, or red Thai curry paste, or
  1 tablespoon (15 mL) of yellow curry powder

2 pounds (1 kg) of fresh baby spinach leaves

A sprinkle or two of salt

Pour the coconut milk and its cream into a large saucepan. Whisk in the curry and bring the aromatic mixture to a boil over medium-high heat. Stir in the spinach and continue stirring just until all the leaves wilt, about 5 minutes. Season to your taste with salt. Serve and share!

KITCHEN TIP

Thai cooks make many fresh curry pastes with many types of chili peppers. The colour of a prepared Thai curry paste indicates its spicy heat level. Yellow curry paste is seasoned without chilies, so it's the mildest. Red is spicy, and green the hottest of all.

LEMON GARLIC-SCENTED BROCCOLI RABE

Broccoli rabe is one of Italy's most prized vegetables and one of my personal favourite greens. Its memorable flavour perfectly balances sweet and savoury, blending earthy floral with pleasingly bitter. The vegetable is quite delicious plain but positively irresistible when perfumed with golden garlic and bright, tangy lemon. **Serves 4**

1/4 cup (60 mL) of olive oil
Cloves from 1 head of garlic, thinly sliced
1/2 cup (125 mL) water
The zest and juice of a lemon
2 pounds (1 kg) of broccoli rabe, trimmed, larger hollow stalks discarded
A sprinkle or two of salt and lots of freshly ground pepper

Splash the olive oil into a medium saucepan with a tight-fitting lid and heat it over medium-high heat. Add the garlic and sauté until it's golden brown and fragrant, 1 or 2 minutes. Pour in the water and add the lemon zest and juice. Simmer until the garlic softens a bit, another minute or two. Add the broccoli rabe, without stirring, and cover tightly. Steam until the broccoli rabe is bright green and tender, another 5 or 6 minutes. Transfer the broccoli rabe and broth to a serving bowl, then season to your taste with salt and pepper. Serve and share!

KITCHEN TIP
The key to this dish's bright flavour is the initial higher heat of the garlic sauté. High heat sharpens the pungent aroma of the garlic, releasing toasty caramelized flavours that the lower simmering heat of the broth then perfumes the greens with.

WILTED SPINACH WITH BROWNED ONIONS AND CARAWAY

This dish involves two steps, one patient, the next much speedier. The sweet-savoury flavours of slowly browned onions scented with Old World caraway form the base for a hearty finish of freshly wilted dark green spinach leaves. Good, and good for you! **Serves 4**

1/4 cup (60 mL) of butter
1 tablespoon (15 mL) of caraway seeds
4 large onions, thinly sliced
1 pound (500 g) of fresh baby spinach leaves
A sprinkle or two of salt and lots of freshly ground pepper

Toss the butter into a small saucepan over medium-high heat, swirling gently as it melts, foams, and begins to brown. Toss in the caraway seeds, then stir for a few moments as they quickly toast and become fragrant. Toss in the onions and sauté, stirring frequently as they begin to release their moisture. Continue cooking, stirring occasionally and lowering the heat as the moisture evaporates and the onions begin to brown and thicken.

When the onions are deep golden brown, after about 20 minutes, add a splash of water, then cram in the spinach. Increase the heat to medium-high, cover, and steam until the spinach wilts and its colour intensifies, just 3 or 4 minutes. Stir everything together with salt and pepper to your taste, then serve and share!

KITCHEN TIP

The vital nutrients in a spinach leaf are released quickly in cooking but lose their vibrancy just as quickly. Dark green micronutrients hit the peak of their intensity as their flavour simultaneously peaks in colour and aroma. On the other side of the curve, they rapidly lose all those qualities, so eat 'em while they're green!

RASPBERRY GINGER RED CABBAGE

Long ago, cooks discovered that a head of sweet red cabbage is a tasty side dish just waiting to happen. A quick stewing is all it takes to unlock the flavour potential of a tightly wound head of cabbage. Simmering with lots of sweet and sour flavours to brighten and balance the cabbage's earthiness doesn't hurt either. **Serves 6**

1 cup (250 mL) of orange juice
1 cup (250 mL) of raspberry jelly or jam
1/4 cup (60 mL) of red wine vinegar
3 tablespoons (50 mL) of grated frozen ginger
1 head of red cabbage, halved, cored, and chopped
A sprinkle or two of salt and lots of freshly ground pepper

In a large saucepan with a tight-fitting lid, combine the orange juice, jelly, vinegar, and 2 tablespoons (30 mL) of the ginger. Bring the sweet-and-sour mixture to a boil over medium-high heat, whisking so the jelly dissolves, then adjust the heat so the liquid is just barely simmering. Toss in the cabbage. Cover tightly and simmer slowly, stirring occasionally, until the cabbage is moist, tender, and flavourful, about 30 minutes.

Stir in the last of the ginger. Season to your taste with salt and pepper. Serve and share!

KITCHEN TIP
As the cabbage stews, keep an eye on the moisture level. If the pot seems to be drying out, just splash in some water. Toward the end of cooking, if it's too watery simply uncover the pot, turn up the heat, and stir as the excess moisture evaporates.

KALE WITH BACON

Kale is one of the heartiest and tastiest greens in the garden; its deep dark green colour signals its intense nutritional density. Kale also has an unmistakable savoury meatiness. Toss in some bacon and you'll have no trouble convincing the carnivores at your table to eat their vegetables! **Serves 4**

8 slices of bacon, sliced crosswise into narrow strips

1 large bunch of kale (about 1 pound/500 g), tougher centre ribs removed
   and leaves chopped into large pieces

A sprinkle or two of salt and lots of freshly ground pepper

Toss the bacon into a large pot with a tight-fitting lid. Cook over medium-high heat, stirring frequently, until the bacon is crispy and brown, about 10 minutes. Spoon out the bacon and drain on a folded paper towel. Pour off most of the bacon fat.

Add a splash or two of water to the pot, then toss in the kale. Cover tightly, reduce the heat to medium, and steam until the kale is tender, about 5 minutes. Season to your taste with salt and pepper. Transfer to a serving bowl and top with the bacon. Serve and share!

KITCHEN TIP

This dish is a great one to show off the very best bacon. Try starting with a chunk of slab bacon cut into smaller pieces. You'll be rewarded with lots of thick, rustic bacon bits.

BACON BEANS WITH BABY SPINACH

White beans and bacon were made for each other. Earthy, dry white beans have to absorb liquid before they can go to the table, so the more flavourful the liquid, the better. This dish hits all the right flavour notes. **Serves 4**

8 ounces (250 g) or so of your finest bacon, sliced crosswise into narrow strips
1 large onion, diced
4 garlic cloves, thinly sliced
1 cup (250 mL) of white beans, soaked overnight in 4 cups (1 L) of water, drained
1 teaspoon (5 mL) of any vinegar
1 pound (500 g) of baby spinach
A sprinkle or two of salt and lots of freshly ground pepper

Toss the bacon into a large saucepan. Cook over medium heat, stirring frequently, until the bacon releases its fat, crisps, and browns, about 10 minutes. Pour off none, some, half, or more of the rendered fat, as much or as little as you like. Toss in the onions and garlic and sauté until they're golden brown and fragrant, another 5 minutes or so. Add the beans and enough water to just barely cover them. Bring to a boil, then reduce the heat so the liquid is just barely simmering. Cover and simmer the beans in the bacon-flavoured broth until they're tender and creamy, about 30 minutes. Just before serving, pour in the vinegar and stir in the spinach until it wilts and shrinks. Season to your taste with salt and pepper. Serve and share!

KITCHEN TIP
Life is about balance—like the decadence of bacon fat balanced with the hearty goodness of nutritionally intense spinach. That's your story. Stick to it.

SPEEDY BLACK BEAN AND GRILLED CORN CHILI

Beyond the full sunny sweetness of a just-boiled freshly shucked ear of corn lies a smoky world of grilled, lightly charred flavour. The perfect accompaniment for that addictive flavour is a complementary vegetable protein–black beans–in this speedy chili! **Serves 4 to 6**

2 tablespoons (30 mL) of vegetable oil, plus more for brushing
1 large onion, chopped
4 garlic cloves, thinly sliced
1 tablespoon (15 mL) of chili powder
1 tablespoon (15 mL) of paprika
1 teaspoon (5 mL) of dried oregano
1 can (28 ounces/796 mL) of chopped tomatoes
1 can (16 ounces/454 mL) of black beans, rinsed and drained
6 ears of corn, shucked
A sprinkle or two of salt and lots of freshly ground pepper
The zest and juice of 2 limes
1 bunch of tender cilantro sprigs, chopped
2 green onions, thinly sliced

Prepare and preheat your grill to its highest setting.

Splash the oil into your favourite large heavy pot over medium-high heat. When it's hot, toss in the onion and garlic and sauté until they're golden and fragrant, 5 minutes or so. Stir in the chili powder, paprika, and oregano. Continue sautéing for another minute or two, gently heating and toasting the spices. Pour in the tomatoes and beans. Bring the mixture to a boil, then reduce the heat so the chili maintains a steady simmer. Simmer, stirring occasionally as the chili thickens, about 20 minutes.

Meanwhile, grill the corn. Coat the ears lightly with oil and season to your taste with salt and pepper. Grill, turning once or twice, until tender, fragrant, and lightly charred, about 10 minutes. Transfer to a plate.

When the grilled ears of corn are cool enough to handle and the chili has thickened nicely, it's time to finish the dish. Season the chili to your taste with salt and pepper. Ladle it into festive bowls. Shave an ear of corn onto each bowl. Top with the lime zest and juice, cilantro, and green onions. Serve and share!

KITCHEN TIP

This dish is considered vegetarian because the classic combination of corn and black beans combines a grain and a legume. Together they not only contain complementary vegetable proteins but are also wildly healthy, hearty, and flavourful.

OLD-SCHOOL FRENCH LENTILS

I love the hearty earthiness of lentils—they are one of my all-time favourite flavours. They may be dressed up in lots of ways, but they're at their best when they're prepared simply so their rustic flavour can shine through. **Serves 4 to 6**

1 tablespoon (15 mL) of olive oil
2 carrots, peeled and finely chopped
1 large onion, minced
4 garlic cloves, minced
1 cup (250 mL) of green lentils
2 cups (500 mL) of water or chicken broth
1 teaspoon (5 mL) of dried thyme
The zest and juice of a lemon
2 tablespoons (30 mL) of minced fresh parsley
A sprinkle or two of salt and lots of freshly ground pepper

In your favourite medium saucepan, heat the oil over medium-high heat. Toss in the carrots, onion, and garlic and sauté until the veggies soften and lightly brown, about 10 minutes. Stir in the lentils, broth, and thyme. Bring to a boil, then reduce the heat so the liquid is barely simmering. Cover and simmer until the lentils are tender, about 30 minutes.

Stir in the lemon zest, lemon juice, and parsley. Season to your taste with salt and pepper. Serve and share!

KITCHEN TIP

One of the secrets to cooking a legume like lentils is to add a last-second dash of acidic brightness. Lemon juice brightens and balances the earthy flavour of the legume—but use it only at the end. If you add the lemon at the beginning of the cooking process, it will toughen the lentils' thin skin and they'll never cook properly.

TOMATO CHICKPEA STEW WITH FRESH BASIL AND DRIED OREGANO

Chickpeas—aka garbanzo beans—are packed with everyday nutrition and lots of tasty texture. In this dish they're speedily stewed with tomatoes and aromatic oregano, then punctuated with dark green bursts of fragrant whole basil leaves. They're a perfect side dish to get on the table in a hurry. **Serves 4**

2 tablespoons (30 mL) of olive oil
1 large onion, diced
8 garlic cloves, thinly sliced
1 can (14 ounces/398 mL) of chopped tomatoes
1 can (19 ounces/540 mL) of chickpeas, rinsed and drained
1 teaspoon (5 mL) of dried oregano
A sprinkle or two of salt and lots of freshly ground pepper
Leaves from 1 large bunch of fresh basil

Splash the olive oil into your favourite medium saucepan over medium-high heat. When it's hot, toss in the onion and garlic and sauté until they're lightly browned, tender, and fragrant. Stir in the tomatoes, chickpeas, and oregano. Bring to a boil, then reduce the heat so the liquid is barely simmering. Simmer, stirring occasionally, until the stew thickens a bit, about 10 minutes. Season to your taste with salt and pepper. At the last second stir in the basil leaves, preserving their fresh aromatic intensity. Serve and share!

KITCHEN TIP

Oregano and basil anchor the herb flavours of the Mediterranean, where they're indisputably at their best fresh. In your home kitchen, though, the flavour of dried oregano is often more intense than fresh. But this isn't the case with basil. The aromatic intensity of fresh basil leaves will always surpass that of their dusty dried relative.

TUSCAN WHITE BEANS WITH OLIVE OIL AND BALSAMIC VINEGAR

Tuscan cooks are patient. They know time is the simple key to one of the world's great bowls of comfort foods: aromatic white beans slowly simmered with sage until sublimely smooth and full of rustic flavour, then moistened with extra virgin olive oil and balsamic vinegar. I didn't invent this dish, but I sure do like to cook and devour it! **Serves 6**

1 pound (500 g) of white beans, picked over and rinsed
Cloves from 1 head of garlic, peeled and halved
2 bay leaves
Leaves from 6 to 8 sprigs of fresh sage
A sprinkle or two of salt and lots of freshly ground pepper
Lots of your finest extra virgin olive oil
A few splashes of quality balsamic vinegar

Soak the white beans overnight in a few quarts of water. Drain them well and proceed. Alternatively—to speed things up—toss the beans into a pot, cover with water, then bring to a boil momentarily before turning them off and resting, covered, for an hour or so before draining and proceeding.

Toss the white beans, garlic, and bay leaves into a large pot with a tight-fitting lid. Pour in enough hot water to cover the beans by 3 inches (8 cm) or so. Lightly salt the water. Slowly and patiently bring the mixture to a simmer over low heat, then cover and adjust the heat so the liquid just barely maintains a slow simmer. Simmer until the beans are aromatic and tender but not mushy, another hour or so.

Meanwhile, stack the sage leaves on top of each other and roll into a tight cylinder. Slice them as thinly as possible.

When the beans are tender, drain away almost all of the cooking liquid. Discard the bay leaves. Stir in the sage, then season to your taste with salt and pepper. Spoon the beans into bowls. Drizzle a generous splash or two of olive oil and a few sprinkles of balsamic vinegar over each bowl. Serve and share!

KITCHEN TIP

You can begin to coax tenderness into a dried bean by patiently soaking it in water, but it will always need heating to finish cooking and become truly tender. Heat applied at various times and temperatures speeds up and finishes the process. You can aggressively simmer un-rehydrated beans steadily for 2 hours or so, but with speed comes a certain coarseness of texture and flavour. A simpler, more passive approach—soaking the beans overnight at room temperature to first hydrate them—shortens the cooking time they need to tenderize while improving their texture and earthy flavour.

SURVIVE OR THRIVE?

Survive or thrive? With food it's your choice. You can merely eat mechanically, buckling under the perceived pressures of modern life, placidly ceding control to Big Food Inc. You can also choose your own path.

Be alive and thrive! We truly are what we eat, well beyond just the nutritional capacity of our food. The provenance of our ingredients, the flavours we lovingly create, and who we share them with also matter. Don't take food for granted. Engage, then eat. Smart choices feed the body and the soul. Healthy food is healthy for us and for all who help create it.

BROWN BUTTER MASHED CELERY ROOT

The only thing better than a comforting bowl of warm, freshly mashed brown butter potatoes is the same bowl full of celery root finished the same way. Mashing is a great way to get to know this root vegetable's distinctive sweet earthy flavour. My favourite root vegetable cooked my favourite way! **Serves 4**

2 large celery roots (about 3 pounds/1.5 kg)
8 ounces (250 g) of butter
1 teaspoon (5 mL) of nutmeg
A sprinkle or two of salt and lots of freshly ground pepper

Peel the celery root, then cut it into large chunks. Steam, boil, or microwave them until they're tender. Drain well.

Meanwhile, melt the butter in a small saucepan over medium-high heat. Gently swirl it as it melts, foams, and begins to brown. Once it begins to foam, watch the colour closely. When it's a deep beautiful golden brown, immediately pour the butter into a bowl. This will quickly lower its temperature and prevent brown from becoming black.

Mash the celery root with the butter and nutmeg. Season to your taste with salt and pepper. Serve and share!

KITCHEN TIP

For butter to brown, its temperature must rise dramatically, more than 300°F (150°C) past room temperature, and the last 25°F (12°C) makes or breaks the whole journey. Butter is 20 percent water. As it melts, its temperature rises quickly but then stalls for a few minutes at 212°F (100°C), the boiling point of water. It'll steam and foam, and eventually all the water will evaporate. At that point, the foam subsides and the butter's temperature begins to rise again. It has a long way to go to reach caramelizing temperatures, but without water slowing it down, its temperature rises quickly. Past 350°F (180°C), the milkfat solids in the butter will colour quickly from golden to brown, but by 400°F (200°C) they're burnt and black. That's why it's essential to keep an eye on the colour and stop the process as soon as the butter is deliciously brown.

NUTMEG ROASTED SWEET POTATOES WITH WILTED BABY SPINACH

This dish is a marriage made in heaven. Ounce for ounce, sweet potatoes and spinach are two of the most nutritionally dense foods you can eat. Sweet potatoes are packed with natural sweetness and are very tasty, especially when roasted, caramelized, and candied. Combined with a basket of fresh baby spinach wilted to a hearty green, the two colourful vegetables are a wildly healthy treat. **Serves 4**

2 large sweet potatoes, peeled and diced
1/4 cup (60 mL) of olive oil
1 tablespoon (15 mL) of nutmeg
A sprinkle or two of salt and lots of freshly ground pepper
1 pound (500 g) of fresh baby spinach

Preheat your oven to 375°F (190°C).

Toss the sweet potatoes with the olive oil, nutmeg, salt, and pepper until evenly coated. Pour them onto a baking sheet and spread them in a thick, even layer. Roast, stirring once or twice, until they're golden brown, tender, and full of sweet and spicy concentrated flavours, about 1 hour. Remove the pan from the oven and stir in the spinach until it wilts and its colour deepens. If necessary, return the pan to the oven for a few minutes, then stir once again. Serve and share!

KITCHEN TIP

Intense colour signals flavour and nutrition. Brightly coloured sweet potatoes and dark green spinach both pack a strong nutritional punch—they're loaded with complex carbohydrates, dietary fibre, omega-3 fatty acids, vitamins, and minerals. The micronutrients in sweet potatoes are hardy enough to endure a slow, flavourful roasting, whereas those in the spinach are at their best when it's freshly cooked and still green—heat quickly deteriorates them. As spinach's colour deepens and darkens from green to grey, it simultaneously loses its nutritional vitality.

OVEN-ROASTED FRENCH FRIES WITH SPICY KETCHUP

Crispy, crusty potatoes are the holy grail of many kitchens. A perfect golden brown crust wrapped around a creamy smooth centre is certainly a noble culinary goal. To get there, though, you don't need to fry. Instead you can toss a load of hand-cut potatoes with a shot or two of vegetable oil and roast them in a very hot oven until they become golden brown. **Serves 4**

4 large baking potatoes (about 2 pounds/1 kg), peeled
1/2 cup (125 mL) of vegetable oil
A sprinkle or two of salt and lots of freshly ground pepper
1/4 cup (60 mL) of ketchup
2 tablespoons (30 mL) of mayonnaise
1 teaspoon (5 mL) of your favourite hot sauce

Preheat your oven to 450°F (230°C). Place a large baking sheet in the oven to preheat as well.

Cut the potatoes into large, thick, evenly shaped strips or wedges. Put them in a bowl and cover with cold water. Soak them for 20 minutes or so. Drain them well, then pat dry between several folded paper towels. Toss the potatoes with the oil and salt and pepper to your taste.

Spread the potatoes in a single layer on the hot baking sheet. Roast, turning every 10 minutes or so, until they're golden brown and fragrant, 40 to 50 minutes in total.

Meanwhile, whisk together the ketchup, mayonnaise, and hot sauce. Pour into a small festive serving bowl. Serve with the fries and share.

KITCHEN TIP

- Soaking the cut potatoes in cold water releases some of their starches, which helps them to brown faster.
- The perfect french fry is normally fried at 365°F (185°C). But since oil transfers heat much more efficiently than air, your oven needs to be much hotter.

HONEY THYME ROASTED CARROTS AND PARSNIPS

I love the hearty, earthy flavours of root vegetables. Mother Nature stores sugar in them so they're naturally sweet. You can make them even sweeter by roasting and caramelizing them. **Serves 4 to 6**

1 pound (500 g) of large carrots, peeled and sliced 1/2-inch (1 cm) thick on an angle

1 pound (500 g) of parsnips, given the carrot treatment

2 tablespoons (30 mL) of vegetable oil

2 tablespoons (30 mL) of honey

2 tablespoons (30 mL) of water

A sprinkle or two of salt and lots of freshly ground pepper

1 tablespoon (15 mL) of minced fresh thyme

2 green onions, thinly sliced

Preheat your oven to 350°F (190°C).

Toss the carrots, parsnips, oil, honey, and water together. Season to your taste with salt and pepper. Transfer to a large baking dish and roast, stirring once or twice, until the veggies are lightly caramelized and deeply flavoured, about 45 minutes. At the last second stir in the thyme and green onions. Serve and share!

KITCHEN TIP

Within the range of caramelizing temperatures, 350°F (190°C) is relatively low but perfect for this deeply flavoured dish. At this heat, the heartier root vegetables have time to soften as their surface browns. Any higher and the big chunks would burn before they had a chance to tenderize.

MASHED POTATOES WITH ROASTED GARLIC OLIVE OIL

Plain old mashed potatoes are one of the all-time great comfort foods, but this classic dish is also excellent for experimenting beyond just plain butter. Not that there's anything wrong with butter, but olive oil is very flavourful too—especially with roasted garlic. **Serves 4**

4 heads of garlic
1/2 cup (125 mL) of extra virgin olive oil
6 medium baking potatoes, peeled and cut into large chunks
A sprinkle or two of salt and lots of freshly ground pepper

Preheat your oven to 350°F (190°C).

Tightly wrap each head of garlic in foil. Roast until they're tender and fragrant, about 45 minutes. Unwrap the garlic, and when it's cool enough to handle, slice off the top third of each head with a serrated knife. Squeeze as much as possible of the creamy roasted garlic into a small bowl. Mash with a fork and stir in the olive oil.

Meanwhile, boil, steam, or microwave the potatoes until they're tender. Drain well, then pour in the garlic oil and mash until smooth. Season to your taste with salt and pepper. Serve and share!

KITCHEN TIP
Roasting garlic removes its pungent strength, revealing lots of smooth, mellow flavour. But if you prefer your garlic flavour stronger, you can instead mince the garlic, then heat it in the oil until it's sizzling and golden brown before mashing it into the potatoes.

CORN CAKES WITH
AVOCADO CILANTRO SALSA

These crispy golden corn cakes are one of the first dishes I create with the first corn of the season. They're an annual treat that's just as easy to make as pancakes. Top them off with zesty avocado salsa and they'll soon be one of your favourites too. **Serves 4 to 6**

1/2 cup (125 mL) of coarse stone-ground cornmeal
1/2 cup (125 mL) of whole wheat flour
1/2 teaspoon (2 mL) of baking powder
1/2 teaspoon (2 mL) of salt
1/4 teaspoon (1 mL) of freshly ground pepper
2 eggs
1/2 cup (125 mL) of milk
1/4 cup (60 mL) of melted butter
The kernels from 2 ears of corn (about 2 cups/500 mL)
A splash or two of cooking oil

FOR THE SALSA

1 ripe avocado, halved and pitted
1/4 cup (60 mL) of your favourite salsa
1 bunch of tender cilantro sprigs, chopped

In a medium bowl, whisk together the cornmeal, flour, baking powder, salt, and pepper, evenly distributing the finer powders among the coarser ones. In a small bowl, thoroughly whisk together the eggs, milk, and butter. Pour the wet mixture into the dry one and stir together until smooth. Stir in the corn. Cover and refrigerate to rest the batter for 30 minutes or so.

Meanwhile, to make the salsa, spoon the avocado into a small bowl. Toss in the salsa and with the back of a fork mash it into the avocado. Stir in the cilantro.

When the batter has rested, preheat your favourite large heavy frying pan over medium heat. Pour in a splash or two of cooking oil, enough to cover the bottom of the pan with a thin film. When it's hot, spoon a large dollop of the batter into the sizzling oil. Add another spoonful near the first, leaving room for expansion. Continue with the remaining batter until the pan is full. Cook, flipping once, until the cakes are golden brown and crispy, about 5 minutes. Top each cake with a dollop of avocado salsa. Serve and share!

KITCHEN TIP

- Coarse stone-ground cornmeal retains more nutrition and flavour than finer grinds. But because of its coarseness, it needs time to hydrate, to absorb moisture from the batter and soften—hence the 30-minute resting time.
- If you're cooking for a crowd (or your pan isn't big enough to cook them all at once), you can make these corn cakes in advance, cover them loosely with a kitchen towel, and keep them warm for 20 minutes or so in a 250°F (120°C) oven.

SAUSAGE SAGE BREAD PUDDING

Next time you invite a roast turkey to your table, try inviting this tasty side dish too. Its familiar flavours will remind you of classic stuffing, while its smooth pudding-like texture gives it a sophisticated upgrade.
Serves 6 to 8

1 loaf of rustic whole-grain bread (about 1 pound/500 g), cut into large cubes
2 tablespoons (30 mL) of olive oil
4 Italian sausages, cut into large chunks
2 large onions, chopped
8 garlic cloves, thinly sliced
6 eggs
2 cups (500 mL) of milk
1 cup (250 mL) of whipping cream or half-and-half
8 ounces (250 g) of grated Parmigiano-Reggiano cheese
1 cup (250 mL) of slivered almonds
1 cup (250 mL) of raisins
2 apples, cored and diced
2 tablespoons (30 mL) of crumbled dried sage
A sprinkle or two of salt and lots of freshly ground pepper
8 ounces (250 g) of grated mozzarella cheese

Preheat your oven to 400°F (200°C). Lightly oil a large baking dish.

Spread the bread on a baking sheet and toast it in the oven until golden brown and crispy, 15 minutes or so.

Meanwhile, make the pudding base. Splash the olive oil into a large heavy frying pan over medium-high heat. When it's hot, add the sausages and brown thoroughly, about 5 minutes. Remove from the pan. Add the onions and garlic and sauté until golden brown and fragrant, another 5 minutes or so. Remove from the heat.

In a large bowl, whisk the eggs. Whisk in the milk, cream, and Parmesan cheese. Stir in the almonds, raisins, apples, sage, sausages, onions and garlic. Season to your taste with salt and pepper.

Stir the toasted bread into the pudding base until every piece is coated well. Pour the mixture into the baking dish, then top with an even layer of the mozzarella cheese. Let sit for 20 minutes or so. Bake until golden brown, about 45 minutes. Serve and share!

KITCHEN TIP
The secret to this dish's flavour is being patient with the bread. Toasting it in the oven adds lots of familiar browned flavour while also drying out the bread so it can easily absorb the flavourful pudding base. Then, resting before baking gives the bread lots of time to absorb the custardy base.

GRUYÈRE MASHED POTATOES

Every now and then I like to splurge a bit and seriously upgrade a simple batch of mashed potatoes. The buttery, nutty flavour of classic Gruyère cheese is an incredible addition to this classic side dish. You'll never look at mashed potatoes the same way again! **Serves 4**

2 pounds (1 kg) or so of baking potatoes (about 4 large), peeled
1 cup (250 mL) of milk, half-and-half, or whipping cream
1 teaspoon (5 mL) of nutmeg
2 heaping cups (550 mL) of grated Gruyère cheese (about 12 ounces/375 g)
A sprinkle or two of salt and lots of freshly ground pepper

Cut the potatoes into large chunks, then steam, boil, or microwave them until tender. Drain well.

Meanwhile, heat the milk and nutmeg until they're just barely simmering. When the potatoes are done, mash in the milk and cheese. Stir until smooth. Season to your taste with salt and pepper. Serve and share!

KITCHEN TIP
Potatoes are best mashed while still steaming hot because cool potatoes tend to become gummy when stirred or mashed. Using hot milk helps prevent this problem.

SMOKED SALMON STUFFED POTATOES

Twice-baked potatoes are always a crowd pleaser, especially when they're stuffed with special-occasion smoked salmon. The neutral earthy sweetness of the potatoes is the perfect base for the stronger smoky salmon and the tangy cream cheese. **Serves 4**

4 large baking potatoes
1/2 cup (125 mL) of cream cheese, at room temperature
6 ounces (175 g) of your favourite smoked salmon
1 cup (250 mL) of roughly chopped fresh dill sprigs, tougher stems discarded
2 green onions, thinly sliced
1 tablespoon (15 mL) of grainy mustard
A sprinkle or two of salt and lots of freshly ground pepper

Preheat your oven to 400°F (200°C). Bake the potatoes directly on the rack until they're tender to the touch, about 45 minutes.

When they're cool enough to handle, cut off the top of each potato, just enough to expose the interior. Spoon the steaming potato flesh into a medium bowl, scraping out as much from each one as you can but leaving the shell strong enough to support the stuffing. Toss in the cream cheese, stirring and melting it into the warm potato. Add the smoked salmon, dill, green onions, mustard, and salt and pepper to your taste, and with a few quick strokes stir everything together.

Stuff the warm potato mixture back into the potato skins. Bake them on a baking sheet until they're heated through again and deliciously golden brown on top, about 15 minutes. Serve and share!

KITCHEN TIP

To the cook go the spoils of cooking. You can snack on the top slices with perhaps a quick drizzle of olive oil, a sprinkling of salt, and a turn or two of your peppermill.

WALNUT WHEAT BERRIES WITH GREEN BEANS AND TARRAGON

Wheat berries have a delightfully firm and chewy texture that easily absorbs the aromas of this brightly coloured salad. This richly textured side dish will add lots of healthy flavours to your table. **Serves 4**

1 cup (250 mL) of wheat berries (whole wheat kernels)
2 bay leaves
2 cups (500 mL) of walnut halves
2 tablespoons (30 mL) of walnut oil
1 tablespoon (15 mL) of red wine vinegar
1 tablespoon (15 mL) of honey
1 tablespoon (15 mL) of Dijon mustard
1/2 cup (125 mL) of fresh tarragon leaves
12 ounces (375 g) of green beans, tough stem end snipped away, delightful tender little curl left intact, halved
A sprinkle or two of salt and lots of freshly ground pepper

Preheat your oven to 350°F (190°C).

Bring a large pot of salted water to a boil. Toss in the wheat berries and reduce the heat so the water is slowly simmering. Toss in the bay leaves and simmer, uncovered, until the wheat berries are tender, chewy, and aromatic, about 1 hour.

Meanwhile, spread the walnuts evenly on a baking sheet and gently toast them in your oven until they're heated through, lightly coloured, and fragrant. Reserve. In a festive salad bowl, whisk together the oil, vinegar, honey, mustard, and tarragon until a smooth vinaigrette forms.

When the wheat berries are done, stir in the green beans and continue cooking until they're bright green and tender, just another few minutes. Drain the wheat berries and green beans well, then add them to the dressing, discarding the bay leaves. Add the toasted walnuts and toss everything together until the salad is evenly coated with the vinaigrette. Season to your taste with salt and pepper. Serve and share!

KITCHEN TIP
Toasting walnuts releases their full fragrance while removing the staleness that inevitably creeps into them during their long, dry transit from tree to table. Toasting always adds flavour!

APPLE-STUFFED ACORN SQUASH

When the seeds are scooped out of an acorn squash, the resulting hollow is custom made for stuffing with other seasonal flavours. The natural sweetness of apples makes them an excellent choice, especially if you quickly stew them with a few savoury flavours. **Serves 4**

4 tablespoons (60 mL) of butter
1 onion, diced
4 garlic cloves, thinly sliced
2 large local apples, unpeeled, cored, and chopped
1 teaspoon (5 mL) of dried thyme
1 cup (250 mL) of apple juice or water
A sprinkle or two of salt and lots of freshly ground pepper
2 acorn squash, halved and seeded
1/2 cup (125 mL) of brown sugar

Preheat your oven to 350°F (190°C).

Toss half of the butter into your favourite medium saucepan over medium-high heat. Swirl the butter gently as it melts and begins to brown. Continue swirling until it's golden brown and fragrant, a few minutes more. Toss in the onion and garlic and sauté until they're lightly brown, another few minutes. Add the apples, thyme, and apple juice. Bring the mixture to a rapid simmer and continue simmering as it stews and thickens, just a few minutes more. Season to your taste with salt and pepper.

Evenly divide the apple mixture among the 4 squash halves. Sprinkle each with brown sugar and top with a pat of the remaining butter. Arrange on a baking sheet and bake until tender, 45 minutes or so. Serve and share!

KITCHEN TIP

You can speed up this dish by stuffing the squash with a few scoops of any pre-made applesauce.

GRILLED ASPARAGUS WITH TARRAGON-STEWED MUSHROOMS

Asparagus, mushrooms, and tarragon are one of my all-time favourite flavour combinations. Throughout my career as a chef I've combined them in many different ways. This is my favourite. **Serves 4**

FOR THE MUSHROOMS

2 tablespoons (30 mL) of melted butter
1 large onion, chopped
4 garlic cloves, thinly sliced
1 pound (500 g) of assorted whole mushrooms, stems removed
1 cup (250 mL) of your favourite dry red wine
2 tablespoons (30 mL) of chopped fresh tarragon
2 green onions, thinly sliced
A sprinkle or two of salt and lots of freshly ground pepper

FOR THE ASPARAGUS

1 bunch of asparagus
2 tablespoons (30 mL) of any cooking oil
A sprinkle or two of salt and lots of freshly ground pepper

Prepare and preheat your grill to its highest setting.

Begin with the mushrooms. Toss the butter into a large heavy frying pan over medium-high heat. Gently swirl it as it melts, foams, and begins to brown. When it's golden brown, toss in the onion and garlic. Sauté until the onion and garlic lightly brown, another 3 or 4 minutes. Toss in the mushrooms and continue sautéing for another 5 minutes or so. Pour in the wine, lower the heat, and simmer, stewing, until the mushrooms are tender and the liquid they release reduces and thickens, another 10 minutes or so.

Meanwhile, grill the asparagus. Splash the oil on the spears and season them to your taste with salt and pepper. Place them crosswise to the grates on your grill. Grill, turning occasionally with tongs, until they're tender and slightly charred, about 5 minutes. Arrange on a serving platter.

Stir the tarragon and green onions into the mushroom stew, season to your taste with salt and pepper, and spoon atop the grilled asparagus. Serve and share!

KITCHEN TIP

Here, great flavour is built in careful, logical steps, each climbing higher: patiently browning the butter, then caramelizing the onion and garlic; slowly simmering the mushrooms to tenderize them and concentrate their flavour; and waiting until the last moment to stir in the sharp tarragon and aromatic green onions, keeping their finishing flavours bright.

GRILLED RATATOUILLE WITH FRESH BASIL

Mediterranean ratatouille is one of the all-time great vegetable dishes. Traditionally it's just a simple vegetable stew of eggplant, zucchini, tomatoes, and bell peppers, but like any stew, how it's cooked affects its final flavour. Tossing everything into a pot and heating it through is fine if you don't mind everything tasting the same. Taking the time to cook the vegetables separately transforms ratatouille into a brightly flavoured dish that retains its individual flavours—especially if you grill them. **Serves 4 to 6**

1 large eggplant, cut lengthwise into 4 thick slices
2 zucchini, halved lengthwise
2 red bell peppers, halved and seeded
4 plum tomatoes, halved
4 green onions
1/2 cup (125 mL) of olive oil
A sprinkle or two of salt and lots of freshly ground pepper
Leaves from 1 large bunch of basil

Prepare and preheat your grill to its highest setting.

Lightly brush the vegetables with olive oil and season to your taste with salt and pepper. Grill, turning once or twice, until tender, fragrant, even lightly charred, about 10 minutes in total. As they finish, toss them into a serving bowl and cut them into smaller pieces, retaining all their tasty juices in the bowl. At the last second add the basil leaves and toss to combine. Serve and share!

KITCHEN TIP

- It's easier to grill a few large eggplant and zucchini slices first and then cut them into smaller pieces rather than the other way round.
- You can grill any tomato, but plum tomatoes have a high ratio of flesh to juices, so they withstand the rigours of the grill best.

PAN-ROASTED ZUCCHINI WITH CHERRY TOMATOES AND OREGANO

Zucchini's firm texture is perfect for the rapid, searing heat of sautéing. A hot pan, a splash of olive oil, an onion, a handful of cherry tomatoes, some aromatic fresh oregano, and a meaty zucchini or two are all you need to toss together a speedy vegetable sauté. You can have this dish on the table in 10 minutes flat. **Serves 4**

2 tablespoons (30 mL) of olive oil
1 large onion, sliced
4 garlic cloves, thinly sliced
2 large zucchini, cubed
1 pint (500 mL) of cherry tomatoes
1/2 cup (125 mL) of chopped fresh oregano
A sprinkle or two of salt and lots of freshly ground pepper

Splash the olive oil into your favourite large heavy frying pan over medium-high heat. When it's hot, toss in the onion, garlic, and zucchini and sauté until golden brown and fragrant, about 5 minutes. Add the tomatoes and oregano and continue sautéing long enough for the tomatoes to heat through and release their juices, another 5 minutes or so. Season to your taste with salt and pepper. Serve and share!

KITCHEN TIP

For the most flavourful results, preheat your pan for a few minutes. If you start with a cold pan, by the time it heats up to searing temperature the zucchini will have cooked through already. If the pan is already hot when the zucchini is added, it can begin searing immediately, and its exterior will brown before its centre cooks through.

CARAMELIZED CAULIFLOWER WITH BROWN BUTTER HOLLANDAISE

You can transform plain white cauliflower into a delicious golden brown treat by simply roasting it. If you're feeling especially decadent, top it with one of cuisine's most luxurious sauces—rich, buttery hollandaise. A well-made hollandaise spooned over anything creates an instant special occasion. It's normally made with plain clarified butter, but for an extra-special treat you can make it with flavourful brown butter. Hollandaise is a bit tricky to make at first, but with patience and finesse you'll successfully add this classic to your kitchen repertoire. **Serves 4**

6 tablespoons (90 mL) of butter
1 head of cauliflower, cut into small florets, centre stalk discarded
A splash or two of vegetable oil
A sprinkle or two of salt and lots of freshly ground pepper
2 large egg yolks
1 tablespoon (15 mL) of cold water
1 teaspoon (5 mL) of Dijon mustard
1 tablespoon (15 mL) of fresh lemon juice

Preheat your oven to 375°F (190°C).

Toss the butter into a small pan and begin melting it over medium heat. Swirl it gently as it begins to foam. Eventually the foam will begin to subside and you'll notice sediment browning in the bottom of the pan. Continue swirling until the sediment turns a deep golden brown. To prevent it from burning, immediately pour it into a small bowl. Rest the butter, swirling it occasionally, until it cools to room temperature. This will take at least 20 minutes or so, maybe longer, and may easily be done well in advance, even the day before. The brown butter may rest at room temperature overnight.

Toss the cauliflower florets with a splash or two of vegetable oil and season to your taste with salt and pepper. Spread in a single layer in a roasting pan and roast, stirring once or twice, until golden brown, 30 to 40 minutes.

While the cauliflower roasts, make the hollandaise sauce. In a small pot, bring an inch or so of water to a bare simmer over low heat. In a glass or metal bowl, whisk the egg yolks, cold water, and mustard until light and frothy. Place the bowl over—not in—the barely simmering water and continue whisking until the mixture thickens and more than doubles in volume, 4 or 5 minutes. Remove the bowl from the heat and whisk for a few moments off the heat to cool it slightly. Slowly trickle in the brown butter, whisking constantly. Add all the browned sediment that has settled to the bottom of the butter. Once the butter has been patiently incorporated, slowly whisk in the lemon juice. If you feel the sauce is a bit too thick, feel free to slowly whisk in a few drops of warm water.

Serve the sauce immediately or keep it warm for a few minutes by covering it and placing it over the warm water once again—this time, though, remove the pot from the heat. Transfer the roasted cauliflower to a serving dish and pour the hollandaise over it. Serve and share!

KITCHEN TIP
One of the tricks to making a smooth hollandaise sauce is encouraging the lemon juice to smoothly suspend in the butterfat. Egg yolks help achieve this because of the emulsifying lecithin they contain. Mustard also contains lecithin and helps stabilize the sauce.

TREATS

CHEWY CHOCOLATE CHIP COOKIES

There are many ways to bake a memorable chocolate chip cookie, but this version emphasizes chewiness. If you prefer your cookies with lots of chewy texture without much crispy brittleness, then you'll love these deeply flavoured and tantalizingly textured treats. **Makes about 18 cookies (depending on size)**

1/2 cup (125 mL) of butter (1 stick), at room temperature
2 cups (500 mL) of brown sugar
1 egg
1 teaspoon (5 mL) of vanilla
1-1/2 cups (375 mL) of all-purpose flour
1 teaspoon (5 mL) of baking powder
1/4 teaspoon (1 mL) of salt
2 cups (500 mL) of chocolate chips

Preheat your oven to 375°F (190°C). Lightly grease a cookie sheet.

With an electric mixer, beat the butter with the sugar until smooth and creamy. Whisk in the egg and vanilla until everything is combined well.

Whisk together the flour, baking powder, and salt, evenly distributing the finer powders among the coarser flour. Scrape down the butter bowl and gradually add the flour mix, beating just until combined. Stir in the chocolate chips with a spoon.

Scoop out a ball of the dough with a small spoon, roll it briefly in your hand into an even ball, then place it on the cookie sheet. Flatten the ball slightly. Repeat, leaving 3 or 4 inches (8 to 10 cm) in between the balls for the cookies to expand as they bake. Bake for exactly 12 minutes. Cool for a few minutes on the cookie sheet, then remove and cool further on a rack or a folded newspaper. Try at least one while it's still warm and oozing, but for the best texture wait until the batch cools. Serve and share!

KITCHEN TIP

This cookie recipe promotes chewiness in two ways. It calls for a bit more sugar than normal—sugar absorbs moisture and helps the cookies stay soft and pliant. The cookies are also baked quickly and are removed from the oven before the sugar has a chance to fully caramelize. The more caramelized the sugar, the crisper the cookie becomes as it cools.

CARAMEL MILK CHOCOLATE MOUSSE

This is the holy grail of desserts–rich chocolate and aromatic golden caramel in the same treat. Every chef knows that a smooth, luxurious mousse is a revelation. There are few things you can create in your kitchen that are more deeply satisfying and dangerously addictive! **Serves 6 to 8**

1 cup (250 mL) of sugar
4 cups (1 L) of whipping cream
8 ounces (250 g) of milk chocolate, chopped
1 teaspoon (5 mL) of vanilla

Pour a cup (250 mL) or so of water into your favourite small saucepan and sprinkle the sugar over the water, taking care to avoid the inside edges of the pot. Don't stir the sugar! Heat over medium-high heat. The sugar will melt evenly and the water will bubble away. As the sugar syrup begins to lightly colour, gently swirl the pot to help it evenly brown. Be patient. When the caramel is deep golden brown and amazingly aromatic, carefully pour in 1/2 cup (125 mL) of the cream. Turn off the heat and whisk until smooth. Pour the thick mixture into a shallow pan and cool to room temperature, stirring occasionally, about 20 minutes.

Meanwhile, toss the chocolate into a bowl nestled over—not in—a pot of slowly simmering water. Pour in 1/2 cup (125 mL) of the cream. Whisk until the chocolate is just barely melted, then remove the bowl from the heat and continue whisking until the mixture is smooth.

Whip the remaining 3 cups (750 mL) of cream with the vanilla until smooth and soft. Gently pour in the chocolate and the caramel mixtures. Using a wooden spoon or rubber spatula, gently and quickly fold the flavour trio until the mousse is smoothly combined yet still soft and light. Transfer into your favourite serving bowl or fun dessert glasses. Refrigerate until firm. (The mousse may be made a day or two in advance.) Serve and share!

KITCHEN TIP
I normally prefer dark chocolate for my baking pursuits but find that its intense bitterness overpowers aromatic caramel. Milk chocolate's lighter sweetness perfectly balances the pleasing bitterness of the caramel.

DARK CHOCOLATE PEANUT BUTTER CUPS

Who needs a candy factory full of bland almost-flavours? This incredible treat is surprisingly easy to whip together and inevitably addictive. Make these once and they'll become regulars in your repertoire. **Makes 8 treats**

8 paper or foil muffin liners
8 ounces (250 g) of dark chocolate, chopped
1/2 cup (125 mL) of peanut butter
1/2 cup (125 mL) of cream cheese
1 tablespoon (15 mL) of honey
1 tablespoon (15 mL) of vanilla
1/2 teaspoon (2 mL) of freshly grated nutmeg

Put the muffin liners in a muffin pan. Toss the chocolate into a small bowl gently nestled over—not in— a small pot of barely simmering water. Stir until melted and smooth. Turn off the heat. Holding the liners steady in the muffin pan, use a small pastry brush to paint the inside of each muffin liner with a tablespoon (15 mL) or so of the chocolate, giving them a coating thick enough to harden into a strong container but thin enough that you have about a third of the chocolate left over. Set aside the remaining chocolate. Refrigerate the pan until the chocolate hardens and strengthens, about 15 minutes.

Meanwhile, put the peanut butter and cream cheese into your food processor and process until smooth. Scrape down the bowl with a rubber spatula. Add the honey, vanilla, and nutmeg. Process until smooth. Spoon 3 tablespoons (50 mL) or so of the filling into each hardened chocolate cup, taking care to level the surface of the filling to just below the top edge of the chocolate. Refrigerate until the filling is chilled and firm, about 15 minutes.

Return the remaining chocolate to its steamy perch over gently simmering water and stir until smooth yet again. Spoon a thick, even layer of the melted chocolate over each of the cups, sealing the edges and locking in the hidden filling. Refrigerate once again until firm, then peel off the liners. Serve and share!

KITCHEN TIP

Chocolate is delicate. It burns easily. It melts at room temperature, so over direct heat it scorches quickly— hence the insulating steam bath. Match a pan and bowl large enough to keep all of the chocolate directly over the water. If the delicate chocolate is suspended past the rim of the pan, it'll be exposed to the searing heat rising up the outside of the pan. Careful!

CARAMEL POPCORN

If you can resist blindly grabbing a bag of factory treats off a forgotten shelf, then you can pop and stir a bowl full of a deeply satisfying treat. You'll be surprised at how easy this caramel popcorn is to make, but don't be surprised by how much better it tastes when you make it yourself! **Serves 4**

3 or 4 tablespoons (50 or 60 mL) of corn or vegetable oil
1/4 cup (60 mL) of popcorn kernels
1/4 cup (60 mL) of butter (1/2 stick)
1/2 cup (125 mL) of icing sugar
A sprinkle or two of salt

Line a baking sheet with parchment paper. In a large pot with a tight-fitting lid, heat the oil over medium-high heat. Carefully sprinkle in the popcorn in an even layer 1 kernel deep. Continue heating as the popcorn begins to sizzle. When the first few kernels pop, loosely cover the pot with the lid, leaving a vent wide enough for the steam to escape but not so wide that the violently popping corn escapes. The popping will intensify, peak, and then noticeably begin to diminish. When it does, turn off the heat and wait until the popping stops before removing the lid.

Toss the butter and sugar into the popcorn. Turn the heat back to medium-high. Gently stir the popcorn, evenly coating it with the melted butter and sugar. As the pot continues to heat, the sugar will begin to caramelize. Patiently continue stirring until the popcorn is deep golden brown and deliciously fragrant. Pour the popcorn onto the baking sheet and spread it out evenly as it cools and hardens. Serve and share!

KITCHEN TIP

As the sugar heats, it transforms from white and bland to golden brown and aromatic.
Be patient, though. The deeper the colour, the deeper the flavour. Light tan tastes beige!

TRIPLE-TREAT CREAMSICLE MARSHMALLOWS

Homemade marshmallows are an awesome family project. You can do remarkable things with sugar in your own kitchen. Whip and cool it with gelatin and you'll be rewarded with one of the all-time great treats—a tray of freshly cut glistening, fluffy white marshmallows. Then enjoy them with these different tasty crusts.
Makes 24 large marshmallows or 48 smaller ones

2 cups (500 mL) of water
3 cups (750 mL) of sugar
4 envelopes of unflavoured gelatin (1 box or 28 g)
1/4 teaspoon (1 mL) of salt
1 tablespoon (15 mL) of vanilla
1 teaspoon (5 mL) of orange oil

FOR THE CITRUS SUGAR CRUST

1/2 cup (125 mL) of sugar
The zest of 1 lime
The zest of 1 lemon
The zest of 1 orange

FOR THE CINNAMON CHILI CRUST

1/2 cup (125 mL) of sugar
1 teaspoon (5 mL) of cinnamon
1/4 teaspoon (1 mL) of spicy chili powder

FOR THE COCONUT CRUST

1/2 cup (125 mL) of shredded sweetened coconut

Lightly oil a 13-by-9-inch (3 L) baking pan.

Measure 1-1/4 cups (300 mL) of the water into a small pot. Carefully sprinkle in the sugar, taking care to avoid the inside edges of the pot. Without stirring, heat over medium-high heat. The heating water will dissolve the sugar into pure sugar syrup. Continue heating as the water rapidly boils, steams, and evaporates, concentrating the sugar, about 10 minutes.

Meanwhile, measure the remaining 3/4 cup (175 mL) of water into the bowl of your stand mixer. Sprinkle the gelatin evenly over the water. Let the mixture stand, allowing the gelatin granules to rehydrate and swell, about 5 minutes.

Fit your mixer with the whisk attachment and stir the gelatin mixture on the lowest setting. Carefully pour in the hot sugar syrup, taking care to direct the flow away from the sides of the bowl. Add the salt. To cut down on spatter, cover the bowl loosely with a kitchen towel, and gradually increase the mixer speed to the highest setting. Continue whipping until the mixture cools, stiffens, and becomes thick and fluffy, about 15 minutes. Add the vanilla and orange oil. Whip just until evenly mixed. Pour the mixture into the baking pan and smooth into a thick, even layer. Cover and cool until firm. Cut into even cubes.

Sprinkle the coconut on a baking sheet and warm it up for 5 minutes or so until it's sticky; place in a bowl. In 2 separate bowls, whisk together the citrus sugar crust and the cinnamon chili crust. Divide the marshmallows into 3 piles. Working with 1 pile of marshmallows and 1 coating at a time, toss a freshly cut marshmallow in the coating mixture until it's evenly coated. Serve and share!

KITCHEN TIP

Whipping the marshmallow cools the mixture, which encourages the gelatin to firm and strengthen. This in turn helps it absorb air and thus increase in volume.

DOUBLE CARAMEL CRÈME BRÛLÉE

This is the famous signature crème brûlée that I've served in my restaurants. If you're a fan of caramel, then this treat is for you. Not only does it feature the crisp crackly crust that makes crème brûlée so memorable, but the custard base itself is also caramel flavoured. It's also fun (and a lot easier) to make one giant serving and share! **Serves 4 to 6**

1/2 cup (125 mL) of white sugar
1 cup (250 mL) of whipping cream
1 cup (250 mL) of milk
8 egg yolks
1 teaspoon (5 mL) of vanilla
1/4 teaspoon (1 mL) of salt
1/2 cup (125 mL) of coarse raw sugar
Kitchen blowtorch

Preheat your oven to 300°F (150°C).

Pour a cup (250 mL) or so of water into your favourite small saucepan and sprinkle the sugar over the water, taking care to avoid the inside edges of the pot. Don't stir the sugar! Heat over medium-high heat. The sugar will melt evenly and the water will bubble away. As the sugar syrup begins to lightly colour, gently swirl the pot to help it evenly brown. Be patient. When the caramel is deeply golden brown and amazingly aromatic, carefully pour in the cream and milk. Reduce the heat to low and whisk until smooth and simmering again.

In a medium bowl, whisk together the egg yolks, vanilla, and salt. Slowly whisk in a ladleful of the hot caramel mixture. Continue whisking in a ladleful at a time, gradually increasing the temperature of the egg mixture, until all of the caramel is incorporated. Pour the mixture into a shallow baking dish that nestles easily in another larger pan. Add a couple of inches of hot water to the outer pan and place it in the oven. Nestle the smaller pan into the bigger pan. Bake until the custard is firm throughout but still a bit jiggly in the centre, about 45 minutes. Refrigerate until firm, a few hours or even overnight.

When you're ready to serve dessert, evenly sprinkle the raw sugar over the firm custard. Gently tilt the works back and forth to help spread the sugar around. Fire up your kitchen blowtorch and direct the flame at the sugar from a height of 2 inches (5 cm) or so, smoothly moving it back and forth. Watch carefully as the sugar browns, moving the flame away before it blackens. Continue patiently until the entire surface is brown and crisp. For the crispest results serve immediately but you may also rest for a few minutes or even refrigerate for a few hours. Serve and share!

KITCHEN TIP

- Egg yolks are very strong—they thicken the custard—but to perform they require gentle handling, in this case indirect heating. If they're stirred directly into the simmering caramel, they'll immediately scramble. Instead, the hot liquid is added gradually to the eggs until the two temperatures equalize. This is called tempering. As well, a water bath insulates the custard from the direct damaging heat of the oven.

- Gentle heat maximizes the eggs' molecular protein structure, binding the flavourful milk and cream and thickening the custard's smooth texture, but too much heat and the egg proteins overcook, snap, and break into a gritty mess.

KIWI PAVLOVA WITH STRAWBERRY MARMALADE AND ORANGE CREAM

This treat is inspired by one of the most memorable dishes I've ever eaten. I enjoyed it after a warm, sunny afternoon in the vineyards of New Zealand's Central Otago, hanging out with a gang of foodies and a local chef. We created a feast inspired by the winery's garden, but for dessert the winemaker's mom stole the show with the tastiest, chewiest, softest pavlova I'd ever tasted. Kiwis know their pavlova! **Serves 8**

4 egg whites
1/4 teaspoon (1 mL) of salt
1/8 teaspoon (0.5 mL) of cream of tartar
1 cup (250 mL) of icing sugar
1 tablespoon (15 mL) of cornstarch
1 tablespoon (15 mL) of white vinegar
1 teaspoon (5 mL) of vanilla

FOR THE MARMALADE TOPPING

2 cups (500 mL) of frozen or fresh local strawberries (but not the hard fresh supermarket ones)
1 cup (250 mL) of orange marmalade

FOR THE WHIPPED CREAM

2 cups (500 mL) of whipping cream
1/4 cup (60 mL) of icing sugar
1 teaspoon (5 mL) of orange oil

Preheat your oven to low, low 250°F (120°C). Line a baking sheet with parchment paper. Centre an 8-inch (20 cm) plate on the paper and trace a circle around its edge. Flip over the paper.

Fit the whisk on your stand mixer. Beat the egg whites, salt, and cream of tartar at medium speed until the froth firms and easily holds soft pillowy peaks. Slow the works down and add the sugar a spoonful at a time as it quickly dissolves. Increase the speed to high and whip wildly until the meringue forms smooth shiny peaks, another minute or two. Beat in the cornstarch, vinegar, and vanilla. Dollop the meringue onto the traced circle and with a lightly oiled wooden spoon or rubber spatula, smooth and spread it to the edge of the circle, forming a thick, even disc. Bake until the outside is firm and crispy and the centre is soft and chewy, about 1 hour.

Meanwhile, make the toppings. Toss the strawberries and marmalade into a small pot over medium heat and stir until they're boiling and bubbling. Continue boiling until the marmalade thickens and reduces, 10 minutes or so. Pour into a shallow pan and let cool. Whip the cream, icing sugar, and orange oil until thick and soft. Cover and refrigerate.

Remove the pavlova from the oven and carefully invert it onto a 10-inch (25 cm) or larger serving plate. Gently peel off the parchment paper. Cool for a few minutes before assembling. Top with a thick, even layer of the strawberry marmalade, spreading it to the edges. Mound the orange-perfumed whipped cream on top. Serve and share!

KITCHEN TIP

To speed up the process, first whip the egg whites without the sugar. Sugar gets in the way of the vital egg white protein matrix, the foam. It also absorbs liquid, preventing it from evaporating during baking and thus preserving the soft texture of the pavlova.

DOUBLE VANILLA CAKE WITH DOUBLE CHOCOLATE ICING

Of all the fun flavours and flights of fancy possible in the pastry kitchen, this classic combo of old-school vanilla and chocolate is the best. The deep aromatic flavour of extra vanilla in a rich, moist butter cake and the double dark creaminess of chocolate and cocoa just can't be topped. This is an easy cake to make—just give yourself some time to be the hero! **Serves 8 to 12**

12 ounces (375 g) of butter (3 sticks)
2 cups (500 mL) of sugar
4 eggs
1/4 cup (60 mL) of vanilla
4 cups (1 L) of all-purpose flour
4 teaspoons (20 mL) of baking powder
1 teaspoon (5 mL) of salt
1 cup (250 mL) of milk

FOR THE ICING

1 cup (250 mL) of sugar
1 cup (250 mL) of water
1/2 cup (125 mL) of cocoa powder
12 ounces (375 g) of dark chocolate, chopped
12 ounces (375 g) of butter (3 sticks), cubed

Preheat your oven to 350°F (190°C). Butter and flour two 10-inch (25 cm) cake pans.

Fit the whisk on your stand mixer. Vigorously whip the butter and sugar until light and fluffy, 10 minutes or so. Beat in the eggs 1 at a time, then stir in the vanilla.

Whisk together the flour, baking powder, and salt. Add about a third of the flour to the egg mixture and beat at medium speed just until smooth. Beat in half the milk just until smooth. Repeat, making 2 more additions of flour and 1 of milk, beating just until smooth after each addition. Divide the batter between the prepared pans, smoothing the tops to fill the pans evenly. Bake until golden brown and a tester inserted in the centre comes out clean, 50 minutes or so. Cool on racks to room temperature.

Meanwhile, make the icing. In a small pot, bring the sugar, water, and cocoa to a boil, whisking until smooth. Remove from the heat and whisk in the chocolate and butter until they are thoroughly melted and the icing is smooth and luxurious. If it feels too thin, cool, whisking occasionally, until it thickens.

Invert the cooled cakes out of their pans and carefully turn them right side up. Use a serrated knife to trim the cakes so their tops are flat. (Snack on the trimmings!) Place 1 cake on a serving plate, cut side up. With a spatula, gently and smoothly top with about one-third of the icing. Invert and nestle the second cake onto the icing. Smooth the icing oozing out the sides with the spatula. Top the works with the remaining icing, evenly encouraging it onto the sides. Twirl and smooth. If you like, rest the cake and admire it for a few hours. Serve and share!

KITCHEN TIP

For enhanced appearance, try an old pastry chefs' trick. Before icing the assembled cake, spread the top and sides with a thin layer of the icing, filling in any holes and smoothing out the shape. Refrigerate for a few minutes to harden the icing and lock in any crumbs. The remaining icing will cleanly and evenly adhere to the sealed surface.

OLD-FASHIONED DOUGHNUT FACTORY

Revving up a doughnut production system is a treat long before the first bite. Nothing beats doing it yourself, and unfamiliar doesn't mean difficult. It's just as easy to make a lot as a little and to create several different toppings, shop-style! **Makes 36 to 48 doughnut balls**

2 eggs
1 cup (250 mL) of sugar
1 cup (250 mL) of milk
1/2 cup (125 mL) of melted butter
4 cups (1 L) of all-purpose flour, plus more for dusting
2 tablespoons (30 mL) of baking powder
1 tablespoon (15 mL) of nutmeg
1 teaspoon (5 mL) of salt
Vegetable oil for deep-frying

FOR THE HONEY GLAZE

1/2 cup (125 mL) of honey
1/4 cup (60 mL) of water
2 cups (500 mL) of icing sugar

FOR THE CHOCOLATE GLAZE

6 ounces (175 g) of dark chocolate, chopped
1/2 cup (125 mL) of butter
2 cups (500 mL) of icing sugar

FOR THE CINNAMON SUGAR

1/2 cup (125 mL) of sugar
1 tablespoon (15 mL) of cinnamon

Crack the eggs into a medium bowl, toss in the sugar, and whisk until thick and creamy. Pour in the milk and butter and whisk until smooth and blended.

In a large bowl, whisk together the flour, baking powder, nutmeg, and salt, evenly distributing the finer powders among the coarser flour. Pour the egg mixture over the flour mixture, stirring with a wooden spoon until the dough just barely blends together. Refrigerate the soft, sticky dough until it firms, at least 2 hours or overnight.

Put a little flour in a shallow bowl. Lightly dust the dough, a baking sheet, a rolling pin, your work surface, and your hands with flour. Roll the dough out about 1/2 inch (1 cm) thick. Punch out as many holes as you can with a doughnut-hole cutter or small cookie cutter. Roll the rounds in the bowl of flour, then place them on the baking sheet. Press the remaining dough back together and repeat. Rest the balls until they soften and a thin oil-resistant crust forms, 30 to 45 minutes.

continued

Meanwhile, pour 3 to 4 inches (8 to 10 cm) of vegetable oil into a large heavy pot or countertop deep-fryer and heat the oil to 375°F (190°C). As the oil heats up, make the toppings. For the honey glaze, simmer the honey and water together for 5 minutes, then remove from the heat and whisk in the icing sugar until smooth; cool. For the chocolate glaze, melt the chocolate and butter together in a bowl nestled over a small pot of simmering water, stirring until smooth, then remove from the heat and whisk in the icing sugar; cool. For the cinnamon sugar, toss the sugar and cinnamon together.

Carefully slide 10 or 12 doughnut holes into the hot oil, taking care not to crowd the pan. Gently fry the doughnuts, stirring occasionally, until they're golden brown all over, 3 or 4 minutes in total. Cut 1 or 2 in half to gauge doneness. Remove with tongs and drain on folded paper towels. Allow the oil to return to 375°F (190°C), then continue with the remaining rounds. Toss some of the hot doughnuts in the cinnamon sugar. Cool the rest of the doughnut holes for a few minutes before dipping and rolling them in the honey or chocolate glazes. Serve and share!

KITCHEN TIP

- The temperature of the oil is very important: 375°F (190°C) perfectly balances the speed of exterior browning against the slower interior cooking.
- The heat of a freshly fried doughnut melts the cinnamon sugar, helping it adhere, but the other two coatings need relative coolness to adhere with an even glaze.

IRON CHEF SOUTHWESTERN STRAWBERRY SHORTCAKE: CUMIN BISCUITS, AVOCADO WHITE CHOCOLATE MOUSSE, AND STRAWBERRY SALSA

When I challenged Bobby Flay in Kitchen Stadium, this dish was my homage to my competitor's cooking roots. Cumin, spicy heat, and cilantro reflect his palate of bold southwestern flavours and my love of savoury surprises in sweets. **Serves 4 to 6**

FOR THE BISCUITS

2 cups (500 mL) of all-purpose flour
2 tablespoons (30 mL) of sugar
1 tablespoon (15 mL) of baking powder
1 tablespoon (15 mL) of ground cumin
1/4 teaspoon (1 mL) of salt
1-1/4 cups (300 mL) of whipping cream
1 tablespoon (15 mL) of vanilla

FOR THE STRAWBERRY SALSA

8 ounces (250 g) of fresh strawberries, hulled and quartered
1 heaping tablespoon (20 mL) of freshly ground pink peppercorns
Leaves from 1 bunch of fresh cilantro, chopped, a few sprigs reserved
The zest and juice of 1 lime
2 tablespoons (30 mL) of honey
2 tablespoons (30 mL) of your finest olive oil

FOR THE AVOCADO MOUSSE

2 ripe avocados, halved, pitted, and peeled
8 ounces (250 g) of white chocolate, chopped

Preheat your oven to 400°F (200°C). Lightly oil a baking sheet.

Begin with the biscuits. In a medium bowl, whisk together the flour, sugar, baking powder, cumin, and salt. Pour in the cream and vanilla; quickly stir together with a wooden spoon just until a moist dough forms. Fold it in half and press it out, kneading the dough in the bowl a few times until all the flour is gathered up. Lightly dust your work surface with flour. Roll the dough out into a disc about 1 inch (2.5 cm) thick. Cut into 4 to 6 pie-shaped wedges. Place on the baking sheet and bake until golden brown, 15 to 20 minutes.

Meanwhile, make the toppings. Toss the salsa ingredients together and reserve. For the mousse, toss the avocado into the bowl of your food processor. Melt the white chocolate in a small bowl nestled over—not in—a small pot of barely simmering water, stirring gently until smooth. Scrape the chocolate into the food processor and process until smooth. Use immediately or refrigerate until firm.

With a serrated knife, gently slice the shortcakes in half. Top the bottom half with a few spoonfuls of strawberry salsa and a generous scoop of mousse. Nestle the top half of the shortcake on top and decorate with a festive sprig or two of cilantro. Serve and share!

KITCHEN TIP

- Pink peppercorns have just as much aromatic intensity as they do spicy heat. Their floral flavour perfumes this uniquely balanced salsa.
- Cool the avocado mousse and the suspended white chocolate will harden, firming and smoothing the final texture.